Remodeling

Fine Homebuilding
GREAT HOUSES

Remodeling

The Taunton Press

Cover photo: Charles Miller
Back-cover photos: top left, Charles Miller;
top right, Roe A. Osborn; bottom, Jefferson Kolle

BOOKS & VIDEOS

for fellow enthusiasts

First printing: 1997
Printed in the United States of America

A FINE HOMEBUILDING Book

FINE HOMEBUILDING® is a trademark of The Taunton Press, Inc., registered in the
U.S. Patent and Trademark Office.

The Taunton Press, Inc., 63 South Main Street, PO Box 5506,
Newtown, CT 06470-5506
e-mail: tp@taunton.com

Library of Congress Cataloging-in-Publication Data

Fine homebuilding great houses. Remodeling.
    p.   cm.
    "A Fine homebuilding book"—CIP t.p. verso.
    Includes index.
    ISBN 1-56158-235-2
    1. Dwellings—Remodeling. I. Taunton Press. II. Fine homebuilding.
TH4816.F554   1997   97-13777
643'.7— dc21   CIP

Contents

Introduction

Old houses are often filled with charm and great potential. But old houses don't always work well for modern lifestyles—kitchens and bathrooms can be cramped and outdated, and sometimes old houses don't have the spaces available for modern activities. The challenge of a good remodel is to make a house more livable while keeping (or creating) old-house charm.

The 32 remodeling projects showcased in this book were originally selected by the editors of *Fine Homebuilding* magazine for the lessons they teach about how to gracefully combine new construction with an old house. Here you'll see how professional remodelers have converted garages, attics, and even a barn into delightful living spaces. You'll also find dozens of ideas for remodeling kitchens and baths, restoring antique gems, or giving new style to a suburban tract house. Whether you live in a house that is 20 or 200 years old, look no further for a wealth of information and inspiration.

Julie M. Trelstad
Editor, Fine Homebuilding *Books*

A Redwood Remodel

Meticulous trim carpentry adorns a Craftsman-style cabin with cathedral ceilings and a trellised deck

by Julie Erreca & Pierre Bourriague

Redwood inside and out. Paneled in redwood, this high-ceilinged room looks out on a grove of redwood trees in the backyard. The 8-ft. tall French doors and the transom window above them emphasize the lofty feeling of the room and let in daylight to balance the rich, dark paneling. Photo taken at A on floor plan.

The earthquake that stopped the 1989 World Series started a lot of building projects in our neighborhood. We live in the redwood-forested hills just north of Santa Cruz, California, near the epicenter of the Loma Prieta earthquake. Fran Lapides and Bill Jurgens live down the road from us in the town of Felton.

Compared with what happened to many of the nearby houses, the damage to Bill and Fran's place was minimal. Their house remained intact, but the brick chimney came apart during the quake and fell off the side of their house. Bill and Fran wanted their fireplace restored and the house patched up. Because we are a design/build team, we were called in before any plans had been finalized to discuss the scope of the project.

Time for an upgrade—In the 1930's and 40's, Felton was a vacation community of summer homes for folks from San Francisco and San Jose. Bill and Fran's house was typical of the cottages built then. It was small—about 800 sq. ft.— and it had simple batten doors, minimal windows and pine paneling everywhere. The bill of sale, which we eventually found in one of the walls, revealed that the cabin originally had been sold for $1,850.

As we talked with Bill and Fran about their plans for the house, we quickly learned that the couple planned to live in it for the rest of their lives and that enlarging the house would suit them just fine. They also wanted to add an outdoor space where they could enjoy warm summer evenings. The chimney repair soon grew into a full-scale makeover that doubled the size of the house. Our mandate from Bill and Fran was to expand the house and to enrich the finishes, such as the trim, counters, cabinets and floor, yet retain the sense of the house as a cabin. We

Form follows foundation.
In doubling the size of this house, the designers placed new structure atop and beside the old foundation. At the southeast corner, a generous deck expands the living space at the apex of the private and public portions of the house.

Photos taken at lettered positions.

SPECS
Bedrooms: 2, plus a study
Bathrooms: 2
Heating system: Forced hot air
Size: 1,600 sq. ft.
Cost: $125 per sq. ft.
Completed: 1992
Location: Felton, California

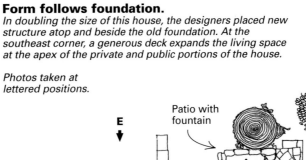

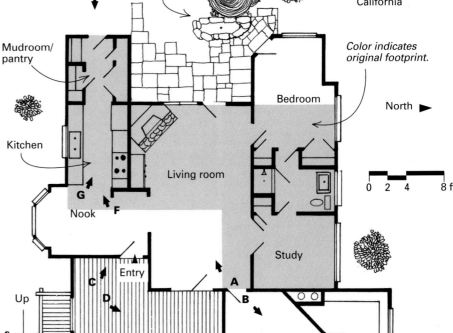

Color indicates original footprint.

A family of gables.
Under a single gable roof, the rooms of this house are topped with cathedral ceilings of varying heights. The result is a collection of rooms with individual personalities, and building them under a single roof simplified weatherproofing the house.

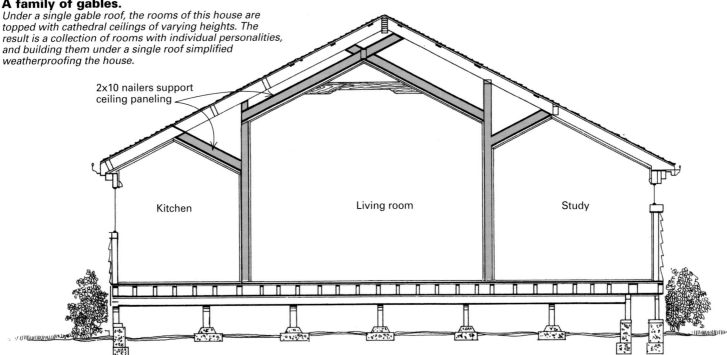

2x10 nailers support ceiling paneling

Kitchen

Living room

Study

Drawings: Andre Junget

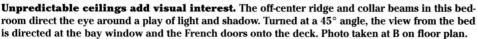

Unpredictable ceilings add visual interest. The off-center ridge and collar beams in this bedroom direct the eye around a play of light and shadow. Turned at a 45° angle, the view from the bed is directed at the bay window and the French doors onto the deck. Photo taken at B on floor plan.

also wanted the house to embody the spirit of the Craftsman tradition, which Gustav Stickley spelled out in a description of a home in *The Craftsman* magazine: "For the spirit of the home is there—the brooding quiet, the sheltering friendliness that comes with simple walls and solid woodwork, pleasant windows that gather air and sunlight, and furnishings that invite to sociability and rest." For us, that meant no drywall: All the walls and ceilings would be paneled in redwood.

New rooms on an old foundation—Bill and Fran's house is on a 10,000-sq. ft. lot that abuts the boundary of Henry Cowell State Park. The house is ringed by redwood trees, some of which are 150-ft. tall. The setback to the park boundary and the restrictions imposed by the local building department meant that an entirely new house could be only about 1,000 sq. ft. A quirk in the

code, however, allows an existing house to be expanded to as large as twice its original size. By retaining the old foundation, we were able to call the project a remodel and build an essentially new house that totals nearly 1,600 sq. ft. We added new spaces to the front and to the rear of the original footprint, carefully tucking new rooms into the spaces between the trees and the side-yard setbacks (floor plan, p. 9).

When a house is surrounded by trees that are more than 100-ft. tall, it needs a high ceiling and plenty of windows to keep it from feeling claustrophobic. And, of course, the dark paneling would make it doubly important to provide daylight at strategic places throughout the house. So at the beginning of the design stage, we made it a priority to give each room a lofty feel and at the same time to make the rooms feel distinctly different from one another.

How high should the ceiling be?—The plan we settled on places the living room at the center of the house. The ridge of this cathedral-ceilinged room is 14-ft. 6-in. high, but it could have been higher. As you can see in the section drawing (bottom drawing, p. 9), the living-room ceiling is well below the gable roof that spans the width of the house. The ceiling boards are affixed to 2x10 nailers on the same pitch as the 6-in-12 roof.

You might ask, "If you want a room to have a lofty feel, why not make it as high as possible?" We lowered the ceiling because if it had been any higher, the room would have lost its sense of intimacy (photo, p. 8). In our experience, if the ceiling gets much taller than 15 ft. or if the wall plate gets higher than 11 ft., the space starts to feel uncomfortable. The wall plate is 11-ft. high in this room, and the room is 17-ft. wide by 25-ft. long. Midway between the wall plate and the

Sculpted timbers surround the deck. To the right of the front door (photo, above), the entry spreads out to create a broad seating area under a trellis. The sturdy trellis structure is designed to support glass panels for yearlong deck use. Photo taken at D on floor plan.

Leaded glass marks the front door. Bordered by a combination trellis and railing, a staircase leads to the front door (photo, right). Where it meets the wall of the house, the horizontal line of the railing is continued as a wainscoting of vertical siding boards. Photo taken at C on floor plan.

The owners use the back door. Screened by a broad overhang, the back door leads to a combination mudroom and pantry (photo, far right). Photo taken at E on floor plan.

A French door leads to the pantry/mudroom. Counterspace is at a premium in a compact kitchen such as this one. So the authors kept most of the food-storage shelves out of the kitchen by placing the pantry in the mudroom at the back of the house. Photo taken at F on floor plan.

Related colors in the kitchen. Redwood is too soft for heavy-use areas such as kitchens, but durable mahogany used instead is nearly the same color. Floors are red oak, stained to match. Coral and black marble covers the counters and wall behind the cooktop. Photo taken at G on floor plan.

ridge, a row of 6x8 redwood timbers imparts a sense of sturdiness and structure to the room. The ends of the timbers are supported by sculpted corbels, and the edges of the timbers are softened with a ⅝-in. radius.

All the doors in the living room are 8-ft. tall by 32-in. wide. This is a particularly pleasing proportion for a four-panel door or a French door, and the doors aren't hard to come by. The Weather Shield doors we used on this job were a stock item at our local lumberyard (Weather Shield Manufacturing Inc., 1 Weather Shield Plaza, Medford, Wis. 54451; 800-222-2995). The extra height of an 8-ft. door dramatically alters the feeling of a room, and in this case the taller French doors at each end of the room let in more light than a standard-height French door. The transom windows over the French doors emphasize the height of the room, let in still more precious light and showcase the view of the redwoods in the backyard.

One end of the living room has a large table for big dinner parties. At the other end a river-rock fireplace by Michael Eckerman dominates the sit-down part of the room. Eckerman's work (see

FHB#82, pp. 88, 89) extends to the backyard, where a small fountain bubbles just outside the French doors. When the doors are open, the sound of falling water can be heard throughout the house. The fireplace design is a stylized horn of plenty, and the fountain includes a fireplace hearth so that people can sit and relax at the side of the waterfall.

Each room has its own cathedral ceiling— There's a Chinese saying that spirits get caught in the corners of shed-roof ceilings. That's probably okay if they're friendly spirits, but we avoid shed-roof ceilings anyway because the eye gets caught in their corners. We much prefer to put cathedral ceilings over a room; they direct the eye up the wall and then back down and around the details much in the way that people would view a painting.

It's not necessary for the ridge of a cathedral ceiling to be centered in the room. In fact, it can add interest to put it off-center, such as the ceiling in the new bedroom (left photo, p. 10). In this room, we further tweaked the typical layout by angling the wall behind the bed at 45° to point

the bed toward the view out the French doors onto the deck.

Enter at the deck—A switchback staircase leads to the front door of the house (bottom left photo, p. 11). The stair is bordered by a picket railing that grows into a trellis as it approaches the door. Where the railing intersects the wall of the house, a band of wainscoting topped with a water-table trim detail extends the horizontal line of the railing around the house.

The deck stretches out from the front door, filling in the roughly 20-ft. square notch in the footprint between the new bedroom wing and the outline of the original house (top photo, p. 11). The deck has several functions. Its sunny location and spaciousness provide the primary outside living area. The trellis off the bedroom was designed to support a glass roof so that the deck can be usable even during the rainy season.

The real entry—There's a good place to park cars right outside the back door, so the rear entry is the one Bill and Fran use most often. For shelter from the sometimes intense winter rainstorms, we extended the roof 48 in. past the wall to act as a canopy over the doorway (bottom right photo, p. 11). This portion of the roof is borne by 4x12 beams that have been detailed with the same stepped profile that shows up on the corbels in the living room and the beams over the deck. The 4x12s, which extend but a few feet into the wall, are supported by 4x8 knee braces.

Just inside the back door is a combination mudroom/pantry. Three closets provide space for supplies, and there is a flip-top bench for sitting to put on shoes and for storing them out of sight. Between the mudroom and the kitchen is another full French door to share the natural light and view between the rooms. For its compact size, the kitchen (photos, facing page) has plenty of counter space because the pantry provides most of the storage.

Colors and patterns—We are lucky enough to be in the heart of redwood country, where several mills are harvesting second-growth and third-growth timber. This wood doesn't have the tight grain pattern of the long-gone old-growth lumber, but it does have other attributes such as variegated colors and bold grain patterns. Fran's love of the wavy-grained redwood prompted the carpenters to select those boards to be used in prominent places, such as the wall under the skylight in the bathroom (photo, right).

All trim boards were routed with a rounded edge to soften their appearance. Also, the edges of boards that abut one another have been rounded over, which accents rather than hides the joints. In addition to trim elements, every beam, fascia and railing were treated this way by our trim carpenters, Craig Johnson, Jeff McGee and Pete Yarwood.

All the interior woodwork on the walls and ceilings is finished with Penetrol, an oil-based finish that has no coloration in it (Flood Co., 1212 Barlow Road, Hudson, Ohio 44236; 800-321-3444). Our painter, Peter Gillett, likes this finish because it's easy to apply, it brings out the richness of the wood and it is easy to clean.

Exterior woodwork (1x8 shiplap k.d. redwood), on the other hand, is finished with a product called Superdeck (Duckback Products Inc., P. O. Box 980, Chico, Calif. 95927; 916-343-3261). This finish has a tiny bit of color in it, which unifies the overall appearance of the siding. Duckback also makes stains that can be used to darken the sapwood that shows up in more and more redwood these days. Just hit the sapwood first with the stain, then go over the whole job with regular finish. Superdeck keeps the red in redwood, so if you want to prevent exterior redwood from turning gray, this product will do the job. It requires annual application.

We chose deep greens as the contrasting trim colors. Because green is the complement of red and the prevalent color of the nearby redwoods, it was tough to imagine any other trim color. Conveniently enough, the dark green Weather Shield windows and doors came prepainted.

When it came time to choose a countertop material for the bathroom, Bill and Fran's innumerable trips to scattered showrooms and dusty warehouses paid off. They found some rich

Skylights help a lot in a wood-paneled house. Bold patterns in dark wood don't mean much if you can't see them. Generous skylights in the bathroom ensure that this deeply figured redwood can be appreciated. Photo taken at H on floor plan.

green granite tiles with black swirls and cream-colored veins in them. We used this tile for the lavatory counter and for the stall shower.

We used coral-colored granite tiles in the kitchen for countertops and the wall behind the cooktop (photos, facing page). As we opened the boxes to inspect the color and pattern of the tiles, we were pleasantly surprised to discover that the tiles were cut from the same slab of granite. Each box was a puzzle in which all the pieces were the same size. So we spread out the tiles,

studied them, and put them back together on the wall and on the counters in the same order they were in when they were sliced out of the earth.

Granite tiles, incidentally, offer substantial savings over granite slabs. They cost on the order of $10 per sq. ft., which is a fraction of the price of a granite slab. □

Julie Erreca and Pierre Bourriague own and operate Bourriague Construction Design in Felton, California. Photos by Charles Miller.

New Life for a Creole Cottage

More windows and fewer partitions help rejuvenate this 700-sq. ft. house built from salvaged river-barge lumber

History was hidden inside. The shape, size and location of this New Orleans cottage suggested that a barge-board house was somewhere inside. New siding, windows and roofing and a picket fence restored its original character. Photo taken at A on floor plan.

by Bruce Goodwin

In Mark Twain's day, traders floated their goods down the Mississippi River to New Orleans on rough flatboats built out of native woods. Without engine power, they couldn't sail their barges back upstream, so they dismantled them and sold the boards for lumber. These "barge boards" became the building material for many small New Orleans houses.

Barge boards are usually about an inch thick and 2 ft. or more wide. The wide surfaces typically show the deep kerf marks of the 6-ft. dia. sawblades used to mill them. Barge-board houses, also called vertical-board houses or box houses, were built like picket fences without studs or posts. The boards were butted edge to edge and fastened with forged nails to sturdy sills at the bottom of the wall and to band beams at the top. Horizontal clapboards, usually of Louisiana cypress, were nailed to barge boards to provide the exterior weathering surface.

The house is covered in time's heavy layers—Built in 1867, the barge-board cottage I bought was covered with several layers of particularly unappealing materials. Not a single splinter of wood was visible on the inside or on the outside. The exterior was covered with aluminum siding (photo above left). Windows were dark-bronze, anodized aluminum. The roof was cement-asbestos shingles. Most of the interior walls were covered with thin, shiny wood-grain hardboard paneling. Ceilings were acoustic tile.

Not only had the house been layered with unattractive materials, it also had been cut into small, dark compartments. Although it was only about 700 sq. ft., the house was divided into six rooms. A couple of plywood closets closed in the spaces even more.

Still, several things about the house appealed to me. It was in a great location on a corner lot

in uptown New Orleans. Plenty of light was available for the eastern, southern and western exposures. The house faced a quiet street that dead-ends a half-block away into Audubon Park. The neighborhood seemed stable and friendly. And it was an eight-minute bicycle ride through the park to my architecture office. The other thing that appealed to me was the house's $35,000 price.

The house sat so close to the property lines that, had I torn the house down, I would have been left with an even smaller buildable area when it was gone. Also, it's the oldest house in the neighborhood, and its historical value was important to me. Although I often regretted it, I decided to work with what was there.

Mapping out a strategy—In such a small house, I decided there should be as few rooms as possible, and most of them should be mini-

mal so that there could be one large space somewhere. And there had to be a lot more light, meaning more and bigger windows and lighter-colored finishes.

In addition, I thought it would be better if the kitchen were on the east rather than the west side of the house (photo left, p. 16) so that it would be sunny in the morning. I also thought that the bedroom should be on the quieter side of the house away from the street.

Putting the design together—The original 19th-century house was a two-room version of a type known as the Creole cottage: a simple pitched-roof rectangle with a central chimney on the interior wall and doors into each room off the porch, which ran the length of the house (floor plans, p. 17). Sometime later, but before the turn of the century, an owner added a shed-roofed space along the north side. More recent-

ly, someone attached and later enclosed a flat-roofed carport at the western end.

The original main rectangle of the house was the obvious candidate for the big space. Besides being in the right place, it had the best exposures and could open up to the tallest part of the roof (photo right, p. 16). In contrast, I laid out the bedroom, bathroom, kitchen and two closets so that they just barely satisfied the required clearances for fixtures, appliances, furniture and door swings. I was able to sneak in a tiny attic space over the hall.

Gutting, reframing and improvising—I did most of the work on the house myself along with veteran carpenter Bill Hickey. We gutted the interior and removed all finishes and non-load-bearing walls. The north-side shed roof sloped down to about 6 ft. above the floor, so we braced it, raised it higher than we would even-

tually want it, reframed the north wall under it and then lowered the roof back down.

In the main room, most of the ceiling joists just rested on the band beams at the top of the side-walls, so they were not really functioning as collar ties for the roof rafters. To raise the ceiling, we took the ceiling joists out and installed two tension-rod assemblies. Each assembly consists of a pair of ⅜-in. threaded rods joined by turnbuckles and coupled to screw eyes at each end. We screwed hooks into the top plates of the walls on both sides of the room and, after slipping the screw eyes onto the hooks, tightened the turnbuckles until the rods were level and tight.

The gable vents are belt-driven attic fans. To reduce heat loss or gain through the louvers, we built trap doors of particleboard with two layers of ½-in. foil-backed rigid insulation board laminated on the inside. The whole assembly is skinned with a sheet of galvanized sheet metal;

More windows and a concrete counter. Many windows take advantage of the kitchen's new eastern exposure. Concrete counters simplify the design. Photo taken at B on floor plan.

One big room instead of several smaller ones. Keeping other rooms small left more room for one large living space. Photo taken at C on floor plan.

each door has a pair of recessed-door cabinet hinges on the top edge and a magnetic weatherstrip all around.

Letting in the light—Originally I had plan-ned to leave the brick chimney in the middle of the big space even though it wasn't functional. But the mortar had turned virtually to dust, and the space felt much bigger when the chimney was gone. We saved the bricks, enough to build a 12-ft. by 12-ft. patio (photo facing page) and a short walk in front.

I hoped to save money and restore a traditional (though not original) appearance by using salvaged-wood windows and doors. The foreman at a local demolition company told me about a house scheduled for demolition in a neighboring city. I wound up buying 12 double-hung windows, the entry set (which we used as

the door from the sunroom to the garden) and six other doors. All were solid tidewater cypress with wide trim and crown moldings. Total cost: $690, screens and delivery included.

Improvising with stock parts—In the kitchen and bathroom, I experimented with materials not typically found in residential interiors. In the bathroom I chose tough, simple fixtures and materials. For lighting I used a pair of inexpensive, surface-mounted exterior boxes and fitted each with two adjustable floodlight sockets and halogen bulbs. A similar system lights the kitchen.

For the bathroom vanity we used 36-in. tall kitchen base cabinets (because I am 6 ft. 7 in. tall), but cut down the depth so that they would not take up so much floor space in the 5-ft. by 8-ft. room. We bought the cabinets and drawers at a local building-supply store, but we made

flush doors and drawer fronts ourselves using edgebanded birch plywood and tab pulls.

Some concrete lessons—We poured a concrete floor in the bathroom, but it was so awkward trying to trowel it smooth in such a confined space that I was unhappy with the surface. After trying to salvage it, I gave up and tiled over it. It felt like a real defeat, but I learned something from it that helped us when we proceeded to the countertops.

I also wanted to make counters and backsplashes out of concrete. We experimented with precasting ½-in. thick backsplashes using Topping 112, a self-leveling wear topping made by Master Builders (Master Builders Inc.; 216-831-5500). We used a heavy-gauge hardware cloth for reinforcement. The surface came out great, but no matter how we coated the forms, we

Left photo this page: Tim Mueller

Kitchen

Bedroom

Bedroom

Dining room

Living room

▲
North

0 2 4   8 ft.

SPECS

Bedrooms: 1
Bathrooms: 1
Heating system: Gas-fired forced air
Size: 700 sq. ft.
Cost: N/A
Completed: 1995
Location: New Orleans, Louisiana

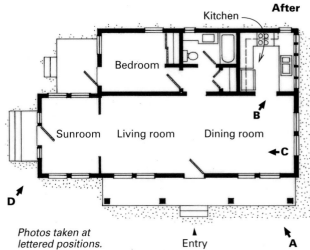

After

Kitchen

Bedroom

Sunroom

Living room

Dining room

B

C

D

Entry

A

The new floor plan makes better use of what's there

Swapping the bedroom and kitchen spaces meant more light in the morning for breakfast, a quieter bedroom and more space for the bath. Removal of the chimney and unnecessary partitions helped to open the house and made a small space feel larger.

Photos taken at lettered positions.

couldn't get the slabs out without cracking them. Eventually, we just went with a painted-wood backsplash.

We decided to pour in place. We put a piece of ¾-in. plywood on top of the cabinets, built a simple plywood form for a square nosing and tacked down an expanded metal screen for reinforcement. Because the topping is about seven times as expensive as a regular bag mix, we poured Quik-Crete to about ¼ in. to ½ in. below the level of the final surface. We then poured Topping 112 for the last fraction of an inch and for the nosing. It leveled itself nicely and yielded a reasonably smooth surface. We made bathroom and kitchen counters this way. ☐

Bruce Goodwin is an architect and professor of architecture at Tulane University in New Orleans. Photos by Steve Culpepper, except where noted.

An outdoor "room" makes a tiny house feel larger. Wooden steps lead from the sunroom to the brick patio, creating the feel of an outdoor room. Photo taken at D on floor plan.

A Remodel in the Spanish Tradition

Plaster detailing seamlessly blends new and old as an architect resolves a poorly organized floor plan

by Jerri Holan

The great Oakland, California, fire of 1991 started a mini building boom in the Bay Area. But not everybody who lost a home built a new one. Some folks chose to take the insurance money and buy older places in nearby neighborhoods. My clients, Lauren Leimbach and Leon Sompolinsky, decided that this approach was right for them. They like the charm of older homes, and they wanted to be in a part of town that still had its landscaping intact.

Their search turned up the almost perfect house. Built in the 20s, their new home is a well-preserved example of the eclectic Spanish style that flourished in California during the 20s and 30s. Its original flavor was intact, with wrought-iron work, leaded windows, a painted wood-beam ceiling and a third-floor veranda. Unfortunately, the house had a befuddled floor plan.

First, the 20s floor plan reflected 20s activities, when meals were prepared in virtual seclusion behind closed doors. The kitchen and the dining room were separate, connected only by a doorway, and they were a half-floor level below the living room. With the ascent of cooking as a social activity, contemporary couples almost always want the kitchen, the dining area and the living room closely connected.

As if to punctuate the irony of the misplaced kitchen, a long, narrow study occupied the space adjacent to the living room (photo right). The two rooms were isolated from one another by a wall of bookcases in the study. Dimly lit and awkwardly proportioned, the study was a kitchen/dining room just waiting to happen. The space even had a pair of French doors leading to the backyard patio.

Freeing the space occupied by the original kitchen would make a perfect place for a guest bedroom. And we could add a shower to the little half-bath off the old kitchen, creating a guest suite without altering the footprint of the original house.

Plaster detailing ties the new work to the old house—The layout of the new kitchen/dining room divides the former study almost exact-

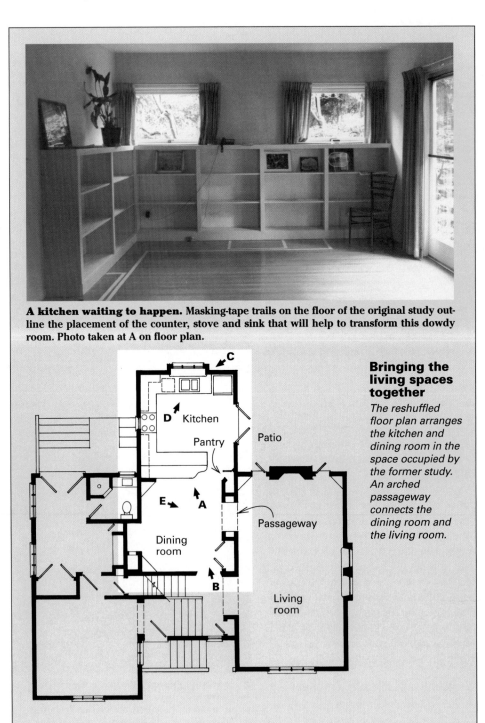

A kitchen waiting to happen. Masking-tape trails on the floor of the original study outline the placement of the counter, stove and sink that will help to transform this dowdy room. Photo taken at A on floor plan.

Bringing the living spaces together

The reshuffled floor plan arranges the kitchen and dining room in the space occupied by the former study. An arched passageway connects the dining room and the living room.

Drawings: Vince Babak. Photo this page: Jerri Holan.

Divided and conquered. The former study is now home to the kitchen and dining room. Plaster details, such as the built-in bookcase on the left, were inspired by living-room bookcases. Above it, a false beam reinforces the separation between the two new spaces. Photo taken at B on floor plan.

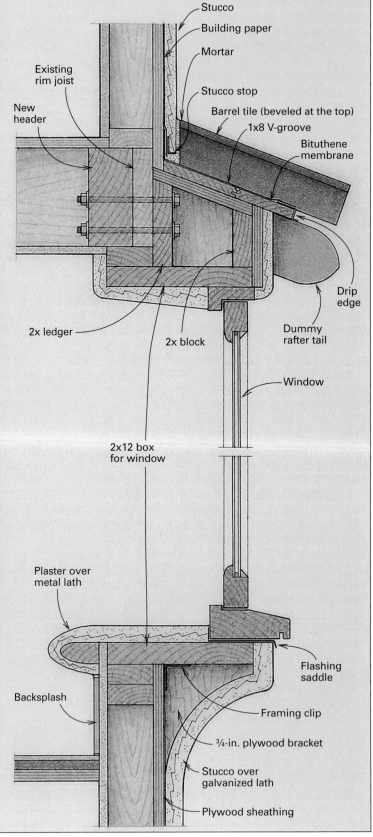

Making room for a tall window

Installed over the kitchen sink, a recycled window overlooks the garden. Note how a new header adjacent to the old rim joist made it possible to bring the window closer to the ceiling, allowing the window to clear the countertop and the tile backsplash.

Stucco

Building paper

Mortar

Existing rim joist

New header

Stucco stop

Barrel tile (beveled at the top)

1x8 V-groove

Bituthene membrane

Drip edge

2x ledger

2x block

Dummy rafter tail

Window

2x12 box for window

Plaster over metal lath

Flashing saddle

Backsplash

Framing clip

¾-in. plywood bracket

Stucco over galvanized lath

Plywood sheathing

Encore for an old window. Recycled from the original kitchen, the window above is set into a shallow bump-out topped with barrel tiles. Photo taken at C on floor plan. From inside (photo below), the deep plaster sill makes a suitable display shelf. Photo taken at D on floor plan.

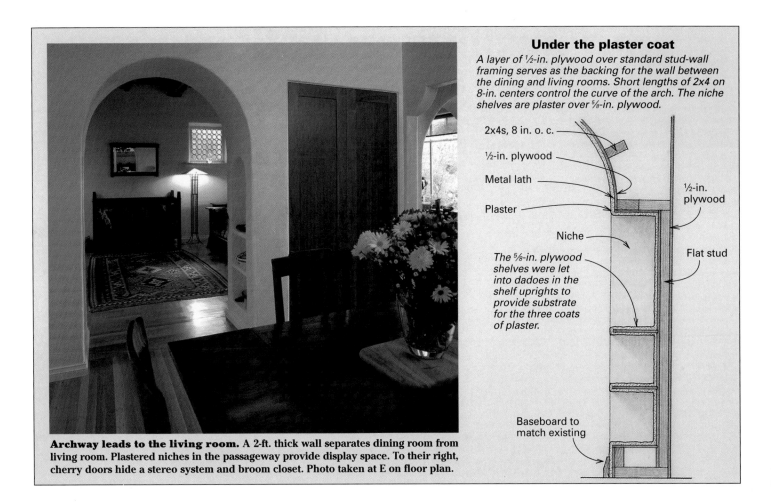

Under the plaster coat

A layer of ½-in. plywood over standard stud-wall framing serves as the backing for the wall between the dining and living rooms. Short lengths of 2x4 on 8-in. centers control the curve of the arch. The niche shelves are plaster over ⅝-in. plywood.

2x4s, 8 in. o. c.

½-in. plywood

Metal lath

Plaster

½-in. plywood

Niche

The ⅝-in. plywood shelves were let into dadoes in the shelf uprights to provide substrate for the three coats of plaster.

Flat stud

Baseboard to match existing

Archway leads to the living room. A 2-ft. thick wall separates dining room from living room. Plastered niches in the passageway provide display space. To their right, cherry doors hide a stereo system and broom closet. Photo taken at E on floor plan.

ly in half lengthwise (floor plan, p. 18). To emphasize this division, we placed a beam across the ceiling at the imaginary boundary between the kitchen and the dining room (photo p. 19). The beam serves no structural purpose. It's there to stake out the border between the rooms and to provide a prominent stage for the curved plaster corbels that tie the beam to the walls. Architectural features such as the rounded corbels in hand-tooled plaster occur throughout the house. They provided us with a rich heritage of detail to duplicate in the remodeled rooms.

For example, the wall between the dining room and the living room (photo above) includes an arched passageway that echoes the original archway in the entry hall. The new wall is 2 ft. thick, providing us with ample room for plastered niches within the new arch. A wall this thick gives the impression of adobe masonry, which was the intent of the original builders of the house. Like the original builders, we made the new wall out of studs, sheathing and plaster. What's not apparent in this remodel is that our contractor, Bashland Builders, used a variety of plaster techniques to achieve the wall finish.

To patch the original plaster in the living room and to create the arched passageway, they used traditional three-coat plaster. This process requires a solid substrate followed by a layer of expanded metal lath and then three applications of plaster (drawing above). This traditional way of applying plaster is labor-intensive, but it's the best method for matching original work and for creating curved surfaces.

The crew used a modern, timesaving bonding agent to speed the plastering of the dining-room walls. Before applying a skim coat of plaster to the old walls, they primed the walls with Plaster-Weld, a bonding agent made by Larsen Products Corp. (800-633-6668). This product ensured that the new plaster bonded thoroughly to the painted surface of the old plaster.

The ceilings of the kitchen and dining room were made with blue board and skim-coated plaster. Blue board is essentially drywall with a porous paper surface designed to grip plaster. The blue board gives the plaster its strength, and a single ¼-in. thick troweled-on layer of plaster provides the hand-worked texture.

A recycled window overlooks the backyard in a bay-window bump-out—It was Leon's idea to reuse the old window. It had to come out of the old kitchen when we put in a pair of French doors to the backyard, and because it came from the shaded side of the house, the window was still in pretty good shape. The downside? The window was warped, and it was too tall to fit into a conventionally framed wall. The window was to go over the sink, which meant that its sill had to be at least 8 in. above the finished counter height.

As shown in the drawing (facing page), contractor Jeff Rexford and his crew placed the new header beside the old rim joist instead of under it. That move saved us the depth of the header, giving us the 4 in. or so of wiggle room that made space for the window. Fortunately, the joists were running in the same direction as this header, so Jeff's crew didn't have to lop off a bunch of joists while temporarily supporting them. Accommodating the warped window meant that Rexford and crew had to plane the window and set the stops accordingly.

The window fits into a 2x12 box supported by four plywood brackets equally spaced below the windowsill. A row of terra-cotta barrel tiles, which match those atop the house, cap the bump-out, and the sides and bottom are stuccoed to match the rest of the house (top photo, facing page). Inside (bottom photo, facing page), the deep windowsill makes a convenient display space and a pass-through counter overlooking the backyard garden. □

Jerri Holan is an architect in Albany, California. Photos by Charles Miller, except where noted.

Transforming an Antique Cape

Rebuilding a chimney in a new location and moving the front door were the keys to a workable floor plan

by Deane Rykerson

A new addition hearkens to tradition. The new cross-gable roof, seen in the center of the photo, joins the house's older sections on the right with the new kitchen on the left. Photo taken at A on floor plan.

The mason spent hours inspecting the old center chimney—checking out the two fireboxes, poking at the withe walls, digging at the foundation. Finally, he declared the chimney unsafe—too far gone for restoration—and he suggested it be torn down. Heeding the mason's recommendation to remove the chimney was the first step toward redesigning the old house.

For months, I had been working on the renovation of this early 19th-century house on an island off the coast of Maine. Razing the old chimney and replacing it in a different location served a better end than just giving the house a new fireplace. It would allow a clear line to be drawn between the purer restoration of the original structure and the more contemporary dining-room addition and kitchen renovation.

To fulfill my client's requirements for a 20th-century summer house, I intended to maintain the 19th-century character of the house while opening up the interior spaces, both to themselves and to the views. The new design would make the house more functional by incorporating a new kitchen, laundry and bath.

Facing the sea and surrounded on three sides by water (photo, facing page), the house is reached by land across a cut-granite-block cause-

A new fireplace improved the traffic flow. The razing of the old chimney allowed a new one to be built in the corner of the living room. The new mantel is appropriate to the original 1830's structure. Photo taken at B on floor plan.

way that crosses a small salt pond. The classical elevation seen from the water was different when approached across the causeway. The old house had a series of worse and worse additions that dribbled off toward the road.

Built by a sea captain—A rumor has it that the house was constructed by a sea captain. Soon after the original structure was built—at the beginning of the 19th century—the sea captain must have prospered because he built a larger, more refined addition to the house with a center chimney and elegant detailing that show early influences of the Greek Revival style, popular beginning around 1830. Still, the oldest parts of the house were broken into small rooms and clearly oriented east, the longest expanse of ocean view.

The first time I walked through the house, it was apparent that over the years past owners had retreated from the deteriorating older parts of the house, building increasingly tasteless additions. The oldest sections were in severe disrepair and virtually abandoned. It seemed as though the beautifully tidy facade seen from the sea was held together with paint. Clearly, the structure, as well as all the mechanical systems, needed work, and the most recent additions and renovations with no relationship to tradition would be demolished.

A new design makes a functional house—The center chimney of the house—the one that the mason had declared terminal—separated the Greek Revival part of the house into two small rooms on the first floor. As is typical with center-chimney capes, the front door opened onto a narrow hall (drawing, left), parallel with the threshold, behind which was the two-fireplace chimney. Behind the chimney, the staircase turned its way up to the second floor (top right photo, p. 24). Removing the chimney opened the first floor into one large living room.

The new chimney was built in a corner of the newly enlarged living room, enabling the room to become the demarcation between the two oldest parts of the house and the more modern addition to the south.

The Greek Revival section of the house was built as a ¾ cape: two windows to one side of the front door and one to the right. After relocating the chimney, the front door opened right into

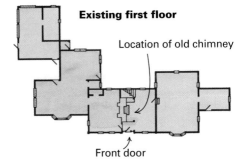

Existing first floor

Location of old chimney

Front door

A renovated cape.
A new dining room under a cross-gable roof connects the old part of the house with the new.

North ▶

0 2 4   8 ft.

Second floor

3

3   8

Dn

3

3

3

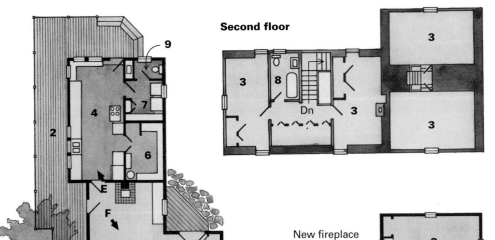

First floor

9

7

4

2

6

E

F

5

C

New fireplace

Up

Up

D

B

1

3

3

8

3

Front door entry

A

Floor-plan key
1 Living room
2 Deck
3 Bedrooms
4 Kitchen
5 Dining room
6 Pantry
7 Laundry
8 Bath
9 Half-bath

Photos taken at lettered positions.

Front door and window were switched. Originally, the house's center chimney was located where the two oak beams cross. Photo taken at C on floor plan.

A two-run staircase became a focal point of the enlarged living room. Photo taken at D on floor plan.

A 19th-century look with 20th-century efficiency. A window seat and breakfast area at the end of the kitchen look out over the salt pond. Glass-front upper cabinets mimic the windows. Blue-painted floors have a top coat of urethane. Photo taken at E on floor plan.

the hearth area of the new fireplace (photo, p. 23), spoiling that space as a cozy sitting area. The solution to the now-constricted traffic flow of the newly enlarged room with its new chimney was simple. We moved the front door to the south and put the window where the door used to be (photo, top left). Doing this maintained the ¾ cape facade while it solved the problem of making an intimate sitting area around the new hearth. Moving the door also brought it closer to the side of the house where the modern additions began and served to make the house appear as a whole rather than simply an old house with new additions.

The view from the land was improved—The land orientation remained a problem. I wanted the house to be attractive from the causeway, yet I didn't want this new elevation to compete with or overwhelm the traditional house. The two older parts of the house had roofs that ran north to south. At some time in the house's history, a barn with an east-to-west ridge had been turned into a hodgepodge of bedrooms. The barn was joined to the old parts of the house by a nondescript (and quite rotten) connection.

I designed a cross-gable dining room to take the place of the nondescript connection. The lines of the cross gable made it seem to stand apart from the old house and made a divergent form visible from the causeway. The cross gables turned the axis of the old house toward the old barn, which would become the new kitchen. Finally, while maintaining the character and scale of the traditional house, the cross-gable roof created a spacious, open dining room with multiple ocean views and a sculptural ceiling (photo, facing page).

The kitchen is modern yet traditional—The kitchen was planned to be efficient and to have views of the salt pond. To increase the feeling of spaciousness in the room, I chose to raise the ceiling of the room up to the rafters. The important design elements were simple: a modular rhythm of cabinets and windowpanes in a large open space with a clear and logical layout.

The kitchen is long and narrow. Along one wall the work area is a long, urethaned Douglas fir counter (photo, bottom left). The other wall is more of a utility wall; it contains the refrigerator, a refurbished 1918 gas-fired cookstove and doors to the pantry and half-bath/laundry area.

A bank of windows over the sink looks out to the pond. Above the long counter, the glass-front upper cabinets mimic the look and feel of the windows. At the end of these two contrasting walls, the house opens again to the outside with west-looking windows and a glass door. This end also incorporates a small, built-in window-seat breakfast area.

The lines of the cabinet doors are simple: square-edge rails and stiles with a flat panel. Most of the storage is in the large pantry, but there is plenty of cabinet storage, including recycling drawers, an essential for island living.

The raised ceiling and antique pendant lights give a good enough angle of light, making under-cabinet lighting unnecessary. The painted

A cross-gable roof connects the old and the new. A high ceiling and banks of windows add to the feeling of spaciousness in the dining room. Photo taken at F on floor plan.

floors are covered with a protective urethane top coat. Painted cabinets give the kitchen a truly 19th-century feel, but they have an underlying 20th-century efficiency.

Windowpane size is important—The windows I used tie together the old and new parts of the house. When we started, all the sashes needed replacement, and I found that Marvin (Marvin Windows and Doors, Warroad, Minn. 56763; 800-346-5128) came closest to replicating the old

nine-over-six double hungs. In the dining room and in the kitchen, we ganged windows to bring in natural light.

Even though the proportion of window size to exterior wall area is greater on the dining room and kitchen additions than it is on the older parts of the house, using windows with the same-sized glass pane gives a continuity to the house's exterior. I find that scaling down architectural components such as doors, windows and moldings in a smaller-scaled addition creates an artificial

miniaturization. If windowpane size can be maintained throughout a house, an addition can relate more successfully to the original structure. With ganged windows in the additions, there is as much natural light in the rooms as one expects in a contemporary home, yet the relationship between the old and the new sections of the house is harmonious. ☐

Deane Rykerson is an architect practicing in Boston, Massachusetts. Photos by Jefferson Kolle.

Details Make the House

Fir woodwork, natural colors and skylights add new flavor to a rebuilt house from the 1920s

by Janet Moody

My husband and I probably aren't the first people who planned on a remodel and ended up with a virtual tear-down. We felt lucky to come across a well-sited old house with a promising backyard. The house had been built on the site of Camp Fremont, which was a World War I army camp about 30 miles south of San Francisco, California, and we lived there for a while before deciding exactly what we wanted to change.

I developed the plans over several years while working in my father's architectural firm and earning my own architect's license. I wanted to make a few adjustments in the floor plan of the 1,680-sq. ft. main house. By adding a second floor for more bedroom space, I could locate my studio on the first floor. But when it came time to

start the project, I discovered that unreinforced concrete footings were cracked or broken and that termite damage in the floor framing was more extensive than I had hoped for. I decided to demolish everything except portions of the living room and the dining room. The rest of the house, from the foundation up, would have to be new.

Finding the original plans—With so little of the original house salvageable, it would have been easy to build a house that was radically different from the original. But by then I was committed to my design. There also was something charming about the original 1920s English-style house with its half-timbering details and clipped gable roof. And a chance discovery in a

book of house plans published in 1924 helped convince me to retain as much as possible of the look and feel of the original house and grounds. The book was a collection of $5,000 house designs, and in it, I came across a plan of my house. The only difference was in two extra rooms, which proved to be later additions. Even the garage and the "poultry yard" and some of the fruit and nut trees were shown in the book just as they appeared at my house.

Retaining old flavor in new construction—In planning the new construction, I kept the timbering detail but extended it all the way around the house. The rough-sawn 2x cedar timbers, standing ⅜ in. proud of the colored stucco walls, help make the house a modern adaptation of a

Original charm outside, new space and light inside. The finished exterior (drawing above) displays the stucco, half-timbering and clipped gables of the original home. But inside, the family/dining room is brightened with new windows, a skylight and a cathedral ceiling. Photo taken from A on floor plan.

Drawing this page: Gary Williamson

Pushing out a wall, adding glass above. A 3-ft. wide bay accommodates skylights. Cutouts in the maple countertop at the far end of the kitchen open to compost and recycling bins. Photo taken from B on floor plan.

Tudor cottage (drawing p. 26). Gable roofs on the main house are clipped back near the peak, just as on the original house. For the roofing, I specified a hexagonal fiber-cement shingle that looked a lot like the roof on an old house in the neighborhood (Supradur, P. O. Box 908, Rye, N. Y. 10580; 800-223-1948).

Under the old paint on the windows and the front door, I found vertical-grain Douglas fir. I especially wanted to keep the old, wavy glass in the windows. I stripped off all of the paint and finished the wood in oil. These details from the old house are complemented by built-ins and woodwork of Douglas fir and floors of recycled pine. And some details give the house its own flavor: a glass-roofed bay in the kitchen, big skylights in the stairwell and two upstairs bathrooms, an exposed-aggregate concrete floor in the master bathroom and a glass-block floor inset in the master bath, which sheds light in a study below.

New space doesn't have to be overwhelming—The footprint of the new building is not significantly larger than the original, so I could preserve yard space (drawing facing page). At the east end of the dining/family room (photo p. 27), I added 3 ft. The kitchen's new skylit bay on the north wall (photo above) also is just 3 ft. wide. On the west end of the house, what had been an old bedroom was expanded by 7 ft. in one direction and 2 ft. in the other to become a studio where I can work. Near the front door, I added 2 ft. 9 in. to the south wall to make room for an entry. In all, the first floor went from 1,680 sq. ft. to 1,969 sq. ft.—not a big increase.

Adding a second floor gave us a three-bedroom 1,063-sq. ft. addition with two bathrooms and a sizable closet and changing area in the master bedroom. What helps make the new second floor and the slight enlargement of the original footprint unobtrusive is the 5-ft. 6-in. plate height at the second-floor walls and exterior details, like

Where compost falls. Cutouts in the kitchen counter help solve the problem of where to stow compost and recyclables. A plastic compost bucket and a full-size trash can in this nook beneath the counter are easily accessed from outside. Photo taken from C on floor plan.

Hallway is lighted from above. An array of three skylights, measuring 9 ft. by 8 ft. in all, lights the stairwell, and the redwood beams dividing the lights add color and remind the author of the house she grew up in. Photo taken from D on floor plan.

No wasted space. Cabinets tucked beneath the stair provide storage space. At the far end of the built-ins is a small work area with a telephone. The floor tiles are linoleum. Photo taken from E on floor plan.

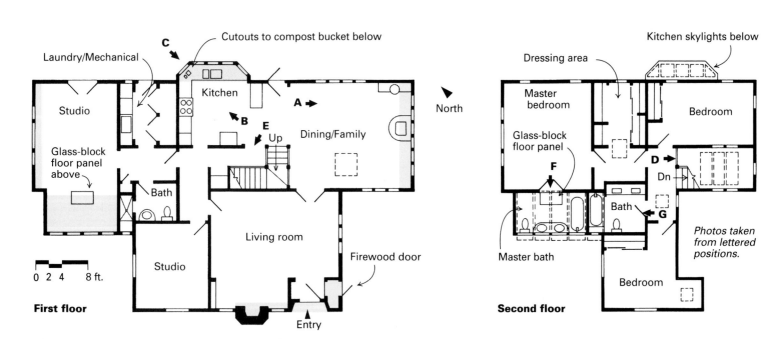

Cutouts to compost bucket below

Laundry/Mechanical

C

Kitchen

A →

North

Studio

Glass-block floor panel above

B

E

Up

Dining/Family

Bath

0 2 4   8 ft.

First floor

Living room

Studio

Firewood door

Entry

Kitchen skylights below

Dressing area

Master bedroom

Bedroom

Glass-block floor panel

F

D →

Dn

G

Photos taken from lettered positions.

Master bath

Bath

Bedroom

Second floor

Small changes in footprint yield big results. *Hoping to retain the feel of the original 1920s house, the author enlarged the footprint only slightly and then added a second floor, nearly doubling the total square footage.*

Shaded areas indicate where the original footprint of the house was expanded. Three banks of skylights—over the master bath, the stairway and the kitchen sink and counter—add substantially to interior light.

A roof of skylights. The master bath is lit from above by a bank of four skylights, each 7 ft. by 3 ft. A glass-block floor panel sheds light to a studio on the first floor. Photo taken from F on floor plan.

Skylight serves two bathrooms. A 3-ft. by 7-ft. skylight, part of the same unit located over the master bath, combines with yellow tiles to make a bright spot of a second-floor bathroom. Photo taken from G on floor plan.

the clipped roof peaks, distinctive roof shingles and half-timbering details that help the new house resemble the original.

Skylights and glass block make it bright and warm—A good deal of the interior light comes from skylights. There are three large banks of them, in addition to the four single units I added. One set, 105 sq. ft. in all, forms the entire roof of the master bathroom (right photo, above), with the last 7-ft. by 3-ft. panel in the frame providing light over the tub and shower in an adjacent bathroom (left photo, above). A second row of skylights, roughly 12 ft. by 3 ft., becomes the roof over the kitchen sink and counter (top photo, p. 28). A third set of skylights is located over the stairwell (right photo, p. 29).

I ordered these nonventing skylights as complete units, not as individual frames that had to

be put together on site. The largest of them, the unit over the master bath, for instance, consisted of a frame set up for five pieces of glass. The anodized aluminum frame was craned into place. Insulated glass was shipped uninstalled, then put into place after the skylight frames were installed.

One word of caution about skylights this large: They generate heat. The south-facing master bath on occasional hot summer afternoons is like a sauna. I've draped cloth and am planning to grow some vines over exposed ceiling beams to cut down on the direct sunlight inside.

In the floor of the master bath is a panel of clear but rippled glass blocks that seemed like a good way of getting light to the studio on the first floor. The panel is directly over my drafting board (for more on how the floor was built, see sidebar, facing page). I also used glass block to form the outside edge of shower stalls in all three bathrooms.

Natural colors make people comfortable—I think most people feel best when they're surrounded by natural elements, so I chose materials and colors that reflect nature. I used water as the theme in the master bath, setting water-worn stones of blue-greens and browns in a concrete bed. To achieve a watery color, I used green slate for the shower walls and base; the polished green-veined black marble on the tub deck and vanity are like placid, reflective water. The large blocks of distorted glass at the shower enclosure also add to the watery sensation. Even the fluorescent desk lamps I used over each of the sinks make contributions. They give a greenish, underwater atmosphere to the room at night.

I used naturally colorful materials elsewhere in the house, too. They include unlacquered copper and brass plumbing fixtures, hardware and trim, terra-cotta tiles in the first-floor bath and the laundry room. There is green marble and slate, red, yellow and orange Persian travertine stone on the first-floor vanity top and orange flagstone in the yard. I also used brightly glazed ceramic tiles in the second bath upstairs (Heath Ceramics, 400 Gate Five Road, Sausilito, Calif. 94965; 415-332-3732) and linoleum squares set in a checkerboard pattern in the kitchen (Forbo Industries, Inc., Humbolt Industrial Park, Maplewood Dr., Hazleton, Pa. 18201; 800-842-7839). Linoleum not only comes in a wonderful marbleized pattern and many colors, but it's also made of natural materials that don't absorb heat.

Woodwork adds visual warmth—My father designed the house I grew up in. It was built entirely of redwood that had been salvaged from an old bridge. I thought it would be pleasing to have something to remind me of that house, so I used redwood beams under the large skylights in the stair hall and in the master bath. When moistened by shower steam, the beams in the bathroom produce a familiar aroma.

Elsewhere, I used Douglas fir for built-in cabinets and trim. The vertical-grain wood has a warm, soft glow. Fir is the material used for the stair railing, and the cutout pattern in the balusters adds a whimsical look to the interior (left photo, p. 29). My 2-year-old son showed me another advantage to the design: The diamond-shaped and round holes provide good handholds for his trips up and down the stairs.

Built-in cabinets below the stairs provide lots of storage in space that is often wasted. One of the drawers serves as a storage bin and dispenser for dog food. Just hold the bowl under the drawer and open a slider in the bottom of the bin. There's even a cubby for the dog's bed. And the space beneath the stair landing is used for extra storage: two big drawers that hold table linen.

Hidden compost—A few details on the outside of the house either make our lives a little easier or add usable space where it might not be expected. Set in the east wall near the entry, for example, is a small door that provides access to a firewood storage bin. From the inside, the door is only a few steps from the fireplace, and the arrangement saves us the trouble of going out the front door to bring in firewood.

Another small door on the back of the house helps solve a minor annoyance common to just about every house: What do you do with the stuff that's headed for either the compost heap or the recycling bin? Open an exterior door in the kitchen bay wall, and you'll find a plastic bucket and a big garbage can in a cavity inside (bottom photo, p. 28). Two small cutouts in the butcher-block counter in the kitchen above provide access. So when we're chopping vegetables in the kitchen, we just pop out a small hatch and sweep the scraps into the compost bucket below. Cans, bottles and other containers to be recycled go into the second hatch. ☐

Janet Moody is an architect living in Menlo Park, Calif. Photos by Scott Gibson except where noted.

Making a floor of small stones

For a look like water. Water-worn stones in blue-greens and browns help give the finished floor in the master bath a serene, waterlike quality. The author started by tracing sinuous designs in a 2½-in. bed of concrete to create swirls of larger stones.

Troweling. Once smaller stones and shells had been sprinkled over the remaining concrete, the entire surface was troweled. The tops of the stones were cleaned later.

Setting the glass-block panel. The 8-in. square glass blocks were set 1 in. above the rest of the cast-concrete frame, allowing room for a border of green slate tile.

Color, texture and light all help give the master bath a tranquil, waterlike atmosphere, and the floor is an important part of the overall effect.

I found blue-green water-worn stones from Malaysia and had them set in a bed of concrete reinforced with 6-in. by 6-in. welded wire. The floor starts with a 2½-in. bed of concrete poured over a ¾-in. plywood subfloor. The thick concrete bed creates the thermal mass for electric radiant-floor heat that I used in both the master bath and the adjoining bathroom. The thickness of the concrete helps prevent cracking.

While the concrete was still wet, I drew a curved pattern for the larger of the two sizes of stones. These stones are up to 2 in. in length, and the flowing lines help give the floor a riverbed effect.

After the larger stones were set, the smaller multicolored stones and shells were sprinkled over the floor to cover the rest of the concrete (top photo, above).

With all of the stones in place, the surface of the floor was troweled (bottom left photo, above). No additional concrete was added. Troweling the surface firmly bedded the stones and brought some of the underlying concrete to the surface. When the concrete had cured, the stone could be cleaned, first with water and then with an acid, to remove all traces of the concrete. The floor subcontractors had rolled on a mixture of Coca Cola and sugar to prevent the top layer of concrete from curing and to make cleanup easier.

The glass-block floor panel was finished flush to the rest of the floor. There are 10, 8-in. square glass blocks in the unit made by Circle Redmont (2760 Business Center Blvd., Melbourne, Fla. 32940; 800-358-3888). Circle Redmont glued the glass blocks onto a steel-reinforced concrete casting and shipped the 400-lb. unit as a whole. I asked that the glass blocks be left 1 in. higher than the surrounding casting. This allowed enough room for a mortar bed and a ⅜-in. thick slate tile surround (bottom right photo, above). The color of the slate helps blend the floor into a unified whole. *—J. M.*

New Life for the Adelman Barn

A glass curtain wall and details inspired by history

by Louis Mackall

A renovation is frequently a conservative thing, as it was in this case. The owners, Bob and Merril Adelman, were quite happy with the existing structure, a 48-ft. long barn attached to their house (the house itself had, until 1947, been a barn; see photo above). Their need was simply to make it usable in the Connecticut winters. Where there were screens over raw openings, we added windows. We added a door with stairs out to the yard, and a cupola for light. Much of the rest involved adding insulation and a new floor. No new interior walls were added; the Adelmans wanted one big room. The trick was doing all this without erasing the patina of age on the inside.

At the outset, it was decided to leave the underside of the gambrel roof untouched so that it could be exposed to the interior. We added 5/4 by 4-in. sleepers, insulation and a new shingle roof on top. This required in-

creasing the fascia depth and fooling around with rigid insulation, but there was no other way that wouldn't have erased one of the most charming aspects of the barn: the interior finish. Where new framing was added to build the cupola, old lumber and old boards for sheathing were used wherever the work would be exposed to view from the inside.

A floating glass wall—The end of the barn had been more or less open for many years, and I wanted to keep the openness (but not the drafts). I was loathe to fill it with conventional windows because of the way their bulky frames would overpower the barn timbers and obstruct the view. The solution, built by Breakfast Woodworks, was to float the window two inches outside the original timber frame and treat it much like a curtain wall (top photo, facing page). The muntin layout was worked out on tracing paper laid over a

measured drawing of the barn end so that timbers and muntins would be synchronized.

We decided to use ⅜-in. insulating glass. The dimension of the muntins was determined by the need to conceal the sealed edges of the glass. We determined that ½-in. deep rabbets would do it (drawing, p. 34). The goal always is to keep the muntin as thin as possible; in this case it's 1⅜ in. thick. We chose the profile to provide enough depth so that the wall would be strong, and chose teak because it required no finish, no maintenance and its color related well with the other parts of the barn. For insurance, though, we applied ⅜-in. by ¼-in. brass flat stock to the interior face of each muntin (photo, p. 34). The strips were fastened to the muntins with Phillips-head brass screws. Among other things, this allowed us to erect the muntins in three sections while maintaining continuity across the joints.

After the wall was up, we tied it into the

Barn again. The main portion of the Adelmans' barn was turned into a house in 1947, and the second, smaller portion covered by this article was renovated recently (photo above). Though a cupola was eliminated in the first renovation, it reappeared in the second. The gable end of the smaller barn features a window wall that draws light indoors; the original timber framing of the barn supports the gable. The remodeling included only the second floor of the barn, leaving the first floor open as an unfinished storage area. Stairs angle up to the entry door (photo right) in order to avoid existing plantings. The Adelmans open the cupola windows in the spring, as the weather warms; hot air is exhausted naturally as cool air is drawn in through lower windows. In the fall, cupola windows are closed for the season.

barn with brass stand-offs screwed to the existing timber frame. These stand-offs allowed us to accommodate differences between the barn frame and our new, straight window wall. The weight of the wall was carried on a separate teak sill anchored with small brackets to the barn. After the muntins were secured, the wall was glazed (photo facing page).

A golden crown of light—Building anything is exciting. I wondered about why this is so for some time and concluded that by building things, we participate in the age-old experience of birth, new life, and all that that means. There is a moment in each project, and indeed in each part of the project, during which that feeling is strongest. For the curtain wall, it was when large sections were assembled on the shop floor, and the wall began to assume the power at which the drawings hinted. For the project as a whole, however, this moment for me was when I first saw the cupola (photos, p. 33).

I had not been to the site for a few weeks. I walked in and of course looked up at the new work; it put a smile on my face that lasted a long time. I recommend cupolas if you enjoy getting high off framing lumber, glass and shingles. Cupolas are as close to pure spirit as one finds in a building.

Satisfying details—One true test of a successful renovation comes when you stand back to look at it. We found this one unusually satisfying, and on reflection, I think there are several reasons. First of all, the look of new wood shingles simply can't be beat. Too, the rake and drip molding came across nicely (drawing right). I had forgotten the visual damage aluminum drip edges have done to the average eave. For this project the builder, Dennis Doyle of Weston, Connecticut, had knives ground to match the existing molding. Molding makes a most wonderful fullness at that important line where the building leaves off and the sky begins. Doyle brought an unusual attention to every aspect of the work, and it shows—we were very lucky to have him on the case.

And there are a couple of likable details at the cupola. One was the angled transition between it and the main roof, and the other was the crisp overhang. But one of the most important elements marking the success of this project came from features given to it by the original builders. The barn had a distinct presence from the time it was first built, as well as strength and a certain scale that is not easily had in this age.

One never quite knows how such a project will turn out, or where it will lead. When things go well, the result is almost always more than anyone would have imagined, because, I suppose, it has had our hearts for a while. □

Louis Mackall is a practicing architect and president of Breakfast Woodworks, Inc. His office and shop are in Guilford, Connecticut.

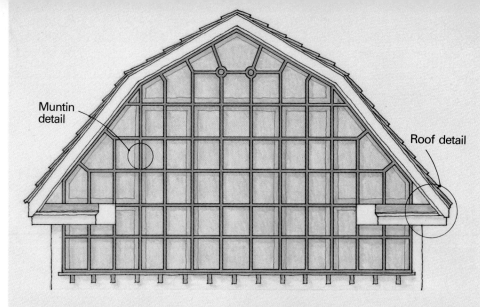

Muntin detail

Roof detail

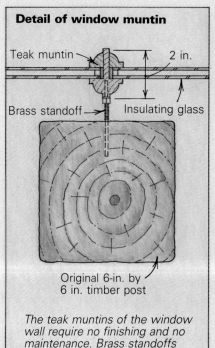

Detail of window muntin

Teak muntin

2 in.

Brass standoff

Insulating glass

Original 6-in. by 6 in. timber post

The teak muntins of the window wall require no finishing and no maintenance. Brass standoffs made from threaded rod allow the windows to float just outside the existing timber frame.

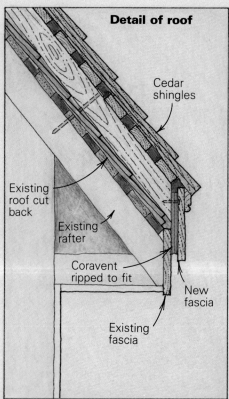

Detail of roof

Cedar shingles

Existing roof cut back

Existing rafter

Coravent ripped to fit

New fascia

Existing fascia

Brass flat stock screwed to the inside of the window muntins (photo above) stiffens the gable-end expanse of glass (photo right). The owners loved the old barn's ceiling, so insulation and a new roof were added above it.

An Arts and Crafts Remodel

A Victorian duplex is gutted and rebuilt for a single family

by Julie Thomas

When the DePaul area became a center of radical political dissent in the 1960s, this house was the Chicago headquarters of the Black Panthers, complete with secret FBI neighbors across the street. As political activity subsided during the 1970s, the neighborhood slid into a period of urban decay, and the house declined along with it.

But the neighborhood's interesting architectural fabric and genteel hipness finally brought urban gentrification, and today the eclectic and prosperous DePaul area of Chicago—namesake of nearby DePaul University—attracts a diverse group of residents.

As scientists—a research scientist and a physician—our clients' exacting natures led them through a systematic survey of options before they hired us to renovate their Victorian in this area on Chicago's near north side.

The couple rented the first-floor apartment of the two-story duplex, or two-flat, in 1978. Five years later, they purchased the house, although for another nine years they continued to live as one of two tenants. During those last two years, they wrestled with the notion of transforming the house into a single-family home.

Because many of their friends had tackled similar large renovations and had scared them with construction horror stories, they first decided to avoid the frustrations and buy a different house. After two years of searching, though, it was clear that no existing house would fit the bill. They called us in early 1992 with a firm commitment to the project and the desire to get going.

The lot is narrow, and the interior dark and cramped—Time had been harsh to the house, inside and out, so there was little worth saving except the stair, and even that eventually got the ax. The house had an original, decorated Victorian facade and poorly constructed front and rear porches, which would have to be replaced. The basement had seen little change since the house was built, and its extremely low ceiling made it seem particularly confining. And there was one problem that couldn't be fixed: Houses similar in proportion and size bound the narrow lot closely on two sides, leaving little or no view and permitting no significant daylight exposure on those sides.

The original structure was typical of the building style. The floor plan of the house was a two-

thirds/one-third arrangement (drawings p. 38). To understand this division, imagine splitting the house lengthwise into two-thirds/one-third slices. As it was, the main living spaces—the living room, dining room and kitchen—all lined up one in front of the other down the two-thirds length of the house. The entry hall, stairway, tiny bedrooms and baths marched front to rear in the one-third section beside these living spaces.

Early in the design process, we decided not to disrupt the structural order for two reasons.

Retaining a large degree of the original framing was cheaper than superimposing a new structural concept on the house. And we also realized that working with the house as is was an opportunity for creative thinking and problem solving. The new floor plan follows the same basic organization, but it allows a modern family to use the house in a modern way.

The benefit of spreading the rooms over two levels is that the once-minuscule bedrooms formerly relegated to the one-third section of the

The entry porch subtly suggests what's to come. Simple Craftsman-style details on the front porch work with the Victorian elements of the facade and suggest what's inside. The house also continues to fit in with the neighboring Victorian houses. Photo taken at A on floor plan.

Warm interior views substitute for the lack of exterior ones. A series of arched doorways and maple-and-cherry portals frames the hallway, which funnels daylight from above into first-floor rooms. The maple floors are inlaid with cherry, a theme that's echoed in the columns leading into the rooms to the right. Photo taken at B on floor plan.

Better use of limited space. *The original one-third/two-thirds floor plan was kept intact. However, the small bedrooms and the add-on* bathrooms in the original house were moved and enlarged as the Chicago-area duplex was converted into a single-family home.

Original house

Second floor

Bed-room
Kitchen
Bed-room
Dining room
Bed-room
← Dn
Living room

First floor

Bed-room
Kitchen
Bed-room
Dining room
Bed-room
Double parlor
Up
▲ Entry

After renovation

Second floor

Terrace
Master bedroom
Walk-in closet
Bedroom
← Dn
Bedroom

First floor

▲ North
Rear porch
Mudroom
D
Family room
Kitchen
Dining room
Living room
Up B
C
A ↗ Entry
0 2 4 8 ft.

Photos taken at lettered positions.

house could occupy the two-thirds portion. In addition, important spaces such as the master bedroom could span the width of the house.

Many years before, our clients had begun an enviable collection of furnishings, lighting and art, a preference for the 19th-century Arts and Crafts style emerging as the common thread among these treasures. So with the given vessel a simple 1870s Victorian house, we set about to design an appropriate background for these objects within its confines.

The interior space is carefully parceled out—Although they were comfortable with the amount of space available in the house, our clients didn't want any square footage wasted or any sprawling suburban-scale spaces.

The frequently used living room was designed in moderate scale that gains some breathing room by being open to the adjacent stair hall (top photo, facing page). The dining room was treated as a dining alcove so that it would not consume valuable space that a busy family could enjoy more fully elsewhere in the house.

The kitchen is positioned in a location that has less than optimum views because it is seldom inhabited during the day. But the kitchen's location adjacent to the family room allows it to borrow light and views from the backyard on weekends and long summer evenings.

The family room houses several functions concurrently. First, it is fitted with a permanent place for two slide projectors and a remote-control pro-

jection screen hidden in a ceiling recess; second, a hidden storage room behind the family-room audio/visual niche stores additional electronics equipment. The house was wired for a remote audio system.

Below, the basement was excavated to a depth sufficient for the 6 ft. 6 in. owner to use it comfortably. Certain auxiliary spaces—a home office, guest suite, wine cellar and child's playroom—occupy the finished portions of the basement. The completed house now comprises about 3,700 sq. ft. over three levels.

Bringing light into a dark house—To maximize privacy, we turned to the interior for views. For example, a view from the front entry is framed by repeating arched doorways and bounded by a series of maple and cherry portals on one side (photo p. 37). This view ends in a final arched niche that contains an antique Hoosier cabinet. Similarly, the living room enjoys a view of the stair framed by one of the portals and its Arts and Crafts style columns.

Despite the lack of exterior exposure to daylight, a mixture of indirect and direct artificial light and daylight from key windows and skylights fills the house. Each portal is fitted with concealed, low-voltage up-lighting. Similarly, the corners of the natural linen and cherry walls in the small dining room pull away to reveal more concealed up-lighting. In the kitchen, some cabinets pull away from the ceiling, revealing a low-voltage lighted display ledge.

Wherever possible, however, daylight is allowed to flood major spaces, especially in the two-story stair hall, where large skylights and undraped windows face south.

Ample sunlight is a plus during long Chicago winters—The skylight penetration through the stair-hall ceiling is fitted with low-voltage up-lighting as well, which provides illumination at night. Softly glowing Arts and Crafts sconces are everywhere, balancing the indirect illumination with direct, subtle lighting. In the master bedroom, a generously sized pair of glass doors with transoms and flanking windows, topped by a soaring, maple-trimmed ceiling, leads onto the second-story terrace. The bed is set into the room's sleeping alcove.

The interior of the house is a composition of natural materials and vibrant colors. The detailing is characterized by a particular element that repeats throughout the house. This element, the tapered cherry column with maple inlay, appears in the portals framing the major rooms and in the newel posts of the stair. The column capital profile, which recalls the spare lines of Stickley designs, also is repeated in the door and window heads and in the cabinets. Also, a raised square of cherry frequently adorns the portals, decorates the kitchen island and punctuates the wall sconces. It is a vestige of the protruding through-tenon common in hand-crafted wood furniture.

The kitchen cabinets (bottom photo, facing page), which form a backdrop to the family

Drawings: Vince Babak

Borrowed light enlivens a dark living room. Although modest in size, the well-used living room gains some breathing room from the adjacent stair hall, which receives daylong indirect sunlight from windows and skylights. Photo taken at C on floor plan.

room, are treated almost as furniture. Each bank of cabinets is an autonomous composition. The island, in particular, with its granite countertop and tongue-and-groove boards, is independent of the remaining kitchen cabinets and sits in perfect symmetry within the view from the family room. Maple floors with cherry inlays, unstained cherry cabinets and cherry trim were chosen to complement the furnishings and artifacts, yet still maintain a livable family home.

The facade is Victorian, but it suggests the Craftsman interior—The owners chose the exterior color scheme after a great deal of research into the appropriate period colors. We designed a new front-entry porch (photo p. 36) that coexists with the original Victorian door and window cornices and the eave brackets. New and existing architectural elements that are part of the Victorian details of the neighborhood were developed or enhanced.

Even though the house was transformed into a single residence, the new front porch retains its original double front door so that the street facade is not disrupted. We chose simple, beveled glass lites in the doors instead of a multiple leaded-glass design because we didn't want any overly ornamented elements to upset the Craftsman-style balance inside. □

Julie Thomas and her husband, Christopher, are architects in Evanston, Illinois. Photos by Steve Culpepper except where noted.

Subtle lighting brings out the warmth of cherry cabinets. Custom-made cabinets, each piece different from the next, work together as individual pieces of furniture. Photo taken at D on floor plan.

Bottom photo this page: John Hollis

Face-lift for a Raised Ranch

Changing the roofline and reshingling the exterior
transform a plain house into
a showplace

by Christopher Hyde

It was a great one-acre lot that held a real dog of a raised ranch. The house looked so bad and was in such poor shape that tearing it down seemed the only way to go. But for reasons of time and economy, the owner decided to work with what he had to try to turn this circa-1970 sow's ear into a silk purse.

The site is about 100 yards from where Edward Hopper stood when he painted the Portland Head lighthouse, which still dominates the scene. Although the house's lot is in a slight depression, from 10 ft. up it offers magnificent views of Casco Bay, the Calendar Islands and Hopper's lighthouse. The lot includes a right-of-way to a sand beach and a mooring in Ship Cove, and the neighborhood is 10 minutes from downtown Portland, Maine.

The existing house, unpretentious to begin with (photo above), suffered from lack of maintenance. Carpenter ants had attacked a second-floor deck. Both the asphalt roof and the exterior-wall shingles needed replacing. Inside, the problems were worse. To increase room sizes, the previous owner removed a party wall running the length of the house on the second floor, which weakened the attic joists. Although the joists had been reinforced, the floor had inches of play at the center.

Quick permitting clinches decision to re-model—Builder John Rousseau, who has remodeled many houses on the Maine coast, often recommends demolition if less than 60% of a house is usable. At first Rousseau thought he could save that much of this shingle-style house. "But as the job progressed, we uncovered more defects; and some of the sound interior details

could not be used for aesthetic reasons," according to Rousseau.

There were, however, solid reasons for working with the existing structure. The foundation was sound and well-oriented. Window locations were only fair, but they were excellent on the seaward side, where several sliding-glass doors opened onto a wraparound deck. The floor plan lent itself to the creation of several large living spaces with sea views.

The barnlike horizontal format of the house would make it possible to add a full third story without making the facade appear as tall as the nearby lighthouse. The new third floor would add about 700 sq. ft. of living space, which would provide a master bedroom and bathroom. Architect Will Pogar of Gauvron Associates Architects found that the total area of the 2,200-sq. ft. house could be expanded by more than 1,000 sq. ft. within basically the same footprint.

Clinching the decision to remodel was the permitting process, which is becoming more difficult and time-consuming for all coastal building. Although it would have been possible to get a permit for new construction, a permit for remodeling was available immediately without planning-board review or other lengthy procedures.

A shingle-style design best suited this remodel—The owner rejected Pogar's initial design for a standard gable with two big dormers as too horizontal. On the second try, Pogar sketched a gambrel roof onto the outline of the ranch and realized a classic shingle-style design was waiting to happen. The second design, with a few modifications, survived as the basis for the project. It permitted the addition of a third story while

maintaining pleasing proportions from the street side, which allowed the house to blend into the neighborhood as the original house had not and which provided the unencumbered interior spaces the owner demanded.

Shingle style is ideal for the Maine coast. The style has a welcoming roofline and shelters large interior spaces. Shingle style also wears well in salt air, shingles weather attractively, and there's a minimum of painted trim to maintain.

Pogar's re-creation honors Maine's premier shingle-style architect, John Calvin Stevens, and uses as much as possible of the original underpinning. With its Doric columns, the front porch is a remnant of a typical shingle-style veranda.

New third story and gambrel roof require beefed-up supports—The final design made four primary modifications to the structure. It added a two-story, 7-ft. by 14-ft. space on the seaward side to enlarge the family room on the first floor and the dining room on the second floor; added a third-floor master bedroom, replacing the original attic; extended the stairwell to the third floor; and drew a slice of the roofline over the garage, which completed the transformation.

Structural analysis indicated that the existing frame could accommodate the weight of the new gambrel roof (right photo, p. 42) if supplemented by 4x16 LVL beams (laminated-veneer lumber) spanning the depth of the house (drawing p. 42). In front, the beams rest on the second-floor walls. In back, two beams bear on 8x8 posts on new footings set outside the existing foundation (left photo, p. 42). Another beam is carried by posts in the walls of the two-story addition. Rousseau cased and shingled the posts to form a

New life breathed into a victim of weather and neglect.

Lack of maintenance and a homely design dictated either tearing down or making over this raised ranch (photo facing page). Fortunately, the barnlike shape of the house, a good foundation and a reasonably sound superstructure allowed upward expansion and the adaptation of the house into a shingle-style showplace (photos above, left).

Top photo: Steve Culpepper

Supporting a third floor and a new roof

New footings outside the old foundation. Posts set on new footings carry the weight of the new third floor and gambrel roof.

A new roof rises from the old. The roofline was raised to make room for additional living and storage space.

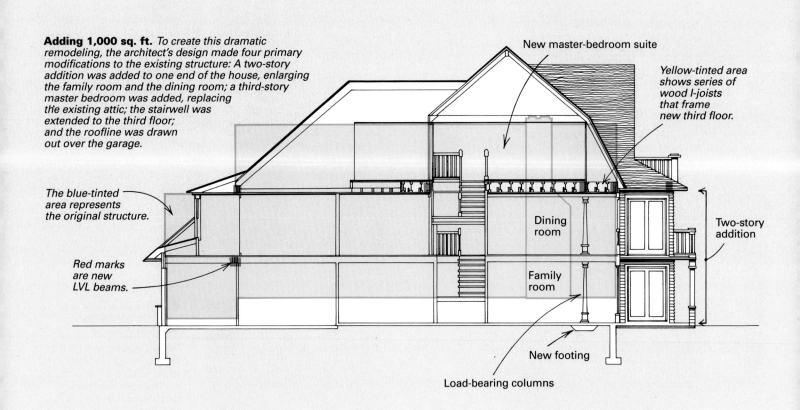

Adding 1,000 sq. ft. *To create this dramatic remodeling, the architect's design made four primary modifications to the existing structure: A two-story addition was added to one end of the house, enlarging the family room and the dining room; a third-story master bedroom was added, replacing the existing attic; the stairwell was extended to the third floor; and the roofline was drawn out over the garage.*

New master-bedroom suite

Yellow-tinted area shows series of wood I-joists that frame new third floor.

The blue-tinted area represents the original structure.

Dining room

Family room

Red marks are new LVL beams.

Two-story addition

New footing

Load-bearing columns

---

double arch beneath the overhanging second story (bottom photo, p. 41).

Although LVLs and 16-in. wood I-joists on 16-in. centers support the third floor, in a 28-ft. span the joists would have an allowable deflection of 0.91 in. at their centers. Because this much deflection would be disconcerting, Pogar specified midspan supports. The centers of the joists and the beams rest on a 6x6 laminated beam supported on the second floor by two 8-in. columns similar to those that flank the front door outside. The architect specified these columns again in the ground-floor family room, where they carry weight to two new footings for the existing slab.

Detailing the exterior—"The shingle style, because of its minimal trim, requires careful spacing of sidewall shingles and absolutely straight courses," Pogar said. "With its variety, it also calls for the ability to cover changes in angle, as on the gambrel-roof pitches; to produce the illusion of a curve; and to cover small areas, such as posts or internal angles, without irregularity." Standard eastern white cedar is sold in several

grades. Rousseau used roof shingles of extra-clear East Coast white cedar, the top grade available, and wall shingles of Maibec extra-clear 5-in. white cedar, resawn, rebutted and predipped in bleaching oil. Rousseau prefers shingles from the Maibec mill. Although they are more expensive than other shingles, shingles milled by Maibec (Industries Maibec Inc., 660 rue Lenoir, Ste-Foy, Quebec, Canada G1X 3W3; 418-653-5280) are kiln-dried and come with a 10-year warranty.

The lowest course of shingles was doubled to start the job, and joints were staggered as far

Drawing: André Junget

away from each other as possible. The layout of courses was determined by the distance between the bottom course and the bottom of the windows, then the top of the windows, and so on, to average no more than 5 in. and no less than 4½ in. to the weather. Rousseau allows ¹⁄₁₆ in. to ⅛ in. between shingles for expansion, although most new shingles are not completely dry and eventually will shrink.

He uses 3d galvanized shingle nails as a rule and lobster-pot nails (1½d galvanized box nails) in exposed situations, such as on the last course under the eaves or on a window apron.

Rousseau and his crew also keep the width of the shingle in mind because wood reacts more across the grain. Therefore, a 12-in. shingle will shrink and swell more than a 3-in. one will. If the shingles are dry, Rousseau's crew allows more space on either side of wide shingles. As a rule, Rousseau scores and splits most shingles over 8 in. or 9 in. because eventually the shingles will split anyway.

Southeast-to-southwest exposures get more sunlight and shrinkage. And shingles on a northern exposure, close to the ground or under eaves never really dry out and need more spacing. Building near the water, as with this house, requires even more care. And Rousseau always looks for the cup, or curl, of each shingle and tries to apply it so that the drying action of the sun will tend to correct it rather than increase the problem. Only two nails are used per shingle, and they're hammered flush but not pounded in tight. The purpose is defeated if the shingle can't move.

Shingling details complete the new look—
To round out the shingle-style look of the house, Rousseau added a slightly flared skirt around the second-floor overhang, and he cased and shingled some of the supporting posts to form shallow arches both in the back and on the porch (photo right).

To build the flared skirt around the house, Rousseau began by nailing up a slightly beveled 2x4. Above that he nailed strapping, and above that he installed a clapboard to finish off the nailing surface for the three courses of shingles, which flare out over the 2x4 shim.

To shingle the arched columns, Rousseau cut plywood sheathing into the curved profile and nailed it onto the posts. Behind the plywood 2x4 diagonal bracing provides a nailing surface for the shingles. Shingles were used to shim out the curve over the 2x4s to create the proper depth. The house's shingling then proceeded as usual with a 5-in. exposure on 15-in. natural (not kiln-dried) shingles.

Each shingle was selected for natural curvature. Outer edges of the shingles were carved with a knife to fit the curve. Where there was a possibility of opening over time, the joint was backed with flashing. Shingles at intersections had to be interwoven, or "married," to maintain aesthetics and to keep them impervious to wind-driven rain. □

Christopher Hyde is a writer in Freeport, Maine. Photos by John Rousseau except where noted.

Throwing a curve into trim design. Proper siding with cedar shingles can create a curve without having to bend the shingles with steam. Shingles that had a natural curve were chosen and nailed to the curved face of the post after it was shimmed out to approximate the curve.

A new entryway carefully tailored to the original form. The local historic commission stipulated that the curve of the portico frieze match the curve of the fanlight above the front door.

Adding a Covered Entry

Designing and building a
sympathetic portico for a 19th-century
New England colonial

by Christopher Wuerth

Adding architectural details to historic houses has been common practice in New England for centuries, but it's always been a tricky business. Building styles change constantly, and early-American design has cycled in and out of fashion. Greek-revival doorways and Italianate porches have been added to 18th-century and early 19th-century homes. In other cases, homeowners have tried to reproduce looks that predate their original houses.

Balancing the owners' tastes with the stylistic requirements of classic New England buildings is often difficult (and sometimes impossible). Luckily on this project, the owners had a great sense of what would work.

My company was asked to add a front-entry portico to a house built in 1826 and located in what is now a historic district of Fairfield, Connecticut. We built the portico on site using mostly stock materials. Our total time on the job, including the design and the construction, was about 90 man-hours.

Starting with a classic colonial—The house has the shape and proportions typical of the area's late 18th-century colonials. The five-bay facade faces the street, and two large brick chimneys flank a central stairway and entry hall. Like many early houses in Connecticut, this one had undergone many changes. Paired Italianate brackets supporting a built-out overhang were added to the main roof in the late 1800s, and windows throughout the house were replaced in the early 1900s with six-over-one lite sash.

The front entryway is composed of a six-panel door flanked by leaded sidelights and capped with an elliptical fanlight, all in the federal-revival style. They were added sometime in the early part of this century.

In deciding how to design and build the new entry portico, we had many factors to consider. There was no evidence in photographs or architectural remnants of what the original portico looked like, if there ever had been one. We had to come up with a design that would fit stylistically and proportionally with the house and at the same time comply with the requirements of the local historic district.

Although there is clear historical evidence that center-hall houses with this type of entry-door surround did not often have projecting porticoes, the owners just as clearly wanted one. We decided to base our design on classical proportions, and then modify it to fit our requirements. Builders in the 18th and 19th centuries commonly used this vernacular approach. Their individual expressions of classic designs, I find, often are the best features of early houses.

We presented the final design to the historic district for review. The plan was approved by the local historic commission with the stipulation that the elliptical arch of the fascia on the new portico follow the curve of the fanlight, and that we not attempt to echo the Italianate brackets of the main house in the soffit of the new portico (drawing right). The owners gave the go-ahead to begin building, leaving the exact molding details and proportions to us.

Paul Curtin, my lead carpenter, and I built the portico. Having Paul to bounce ideas off of always makes a complex job go much faster, with fewer mistakes.

Perspective can improve the view—We worked out the exact design dimensions on paper, marked the outline on the front of the house with chalklines and then stepped back to check the proportions of our lines against the facade. This habit of taking the time to stop, step back and look at what we are doing is one of the most important lessons we have learned from working on old buildings.

After a final check of our measurements and a deep breath, I cut the outline with a circular saw. To our surprise, we discovered an earlier, possibly original wood-shingle layer underneath the top layer of siding, along with the remnants of an earlier doorway. It was an interesting find, but we saw nothing that led us to change our approach. Having cut and removed the shingles, we got a good outline view of the size and proportion of our design.

We decided at this point to rough-frame the entablatures first. This way, we could frame the roof assembly, build the cornice and raking cornice, and get the portico decked and shingled. We would prop it up with 2x4 braces and then install the columns when they arrived.

Durable, weather-resistant materials—Our material choices were fairly simple. Given the small roof size, 2x4 Douglas-fir rafters, 16 in. o. c., were adequate, with ½-in. plywood sheathing. Asphalt roof shingles would match the recently reshingled main roof. For durability and rot-resistance, we chose redwood for the hollow, turned columns (Hartmann Sanders Co., 4340 Bankers Circle, Atlanta, Ga. 30360; 800-241-4303). The column bases and capitals are molded fiberglass, not exactly a traditional material, but durable and indistinguishable from wood when painted.

Historically, these columns would have been made from old-growth eastern white pine. The lumber from these trees was extremely rot-resistant, weathered well, was easy to work and held paint. Almost all of the antique exterior and interior trim, moldings, clapboard siding and roof shingles in our area were made from it. We often find 200-year-old exterior-trim pieces that

were maintained poorly, but the old pine still is in pristine condition.

For this job, we milled some of the trim and architectural elements from 1x12 and 5/4x12 eastern white pine. We can still find some quality New England pine in our area, good enough for exterior work if it will be kept painted but by no means the equal of the early stuff. For moldings, we used stock pine profiles where possible. All wood was back-primed with oil paint before installation.

The two projecting entablatures were laid out using *Practical Elementary Treatise on Architecture* as a guide. This book, by the 16th-century Italian architect Giacomo Barozzi da Vignola, contains intricate scale drawings and descriptions of the five classical orders of architecture. (This book is no longer in print, but Vignola's work has been reproduced in many forms.) Each order is distinguished by its own proportions and decoration. The proportions of the portico were based roughly on the simplest of

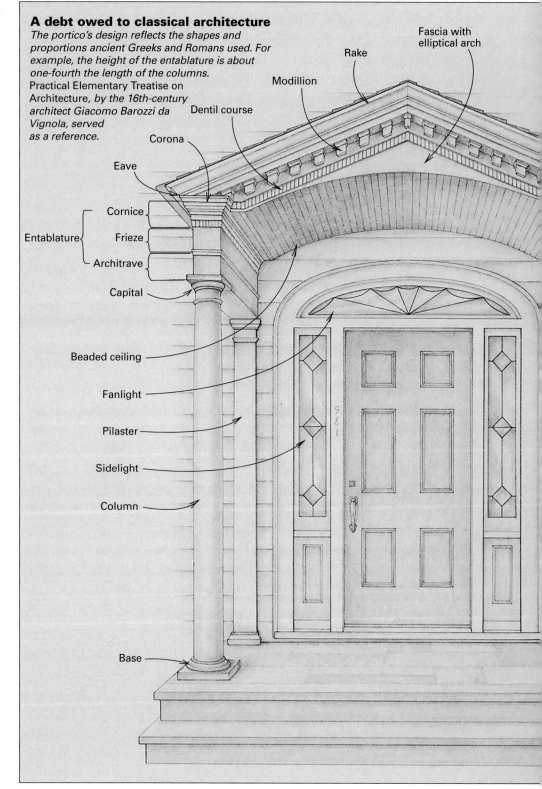

A debt owed to classical architecture
The portico's design reflects the shapes and proportions ancient Greeks and Romans used. For example, the height of the entablature is about one-fourth the length of the columns.
Practical Elementary Treatise on Architecture, *by the 16th-century architect Giacomo Barozzi da Vignola, served as a reference.*

Rake

Fascia with elliptical arch

Modillion

Dentil course

Corona

Eave

Cornice

Frieze

Architrave

Entablature

Capital

Beaded ceiling

Fanlight

Pilaster

Sidelight

Column

Base

The author began building the portico by framing the entablatures. The cedar shingles were cut away to accept the new roof flashing (photo left). Curved collar ties made from 5/4x12 pine boards support the roof framing (photo right) and serve as backing for the beaded ceiling.

the five orders, the Tuscan. Vignola says the height of a Tuscan entablature should be one-quarter of the height of the column supporting it. Using this reference point as our guide, we made the entablature about 20 in. tall. The 2x4 framing for the entablatures was screwed to the house, with the outboard end temporarily propped up (photo top left).

A 2x14 top plate—Each entablature was capped with a 2x14 piece of clear pine trimmed with cove molding. This cap piece, the corona, would act as the wall top plate, simplifying the roof construction and permitting a wide, over-hanging cornice and drip.

The pitch of the portico roof, 5-in-12, was de-termined by existing conditions, including the width of the stoop below and the distance to the window above. The rafters were braced with a temporary 2x4 collar tie while we installed the plywood decking.

Taking a cue from traditional building, we carefully ripped the decking at the edges to pro-vide angled nailing support for the back of the crown molding to be installed later. Period roofs usually were sheathed with full 1-in. thick oak, pine or chestnut roofers. These boards some-times ran by the rafters, and their ends were cut on an angle cut to accept rake-molding nails.

Even good carpenters fudge things occa-sionally—Before we could shingle the portico, we had to complete the cornice moldings at

both the rake and the eave. The plan was to use stock 4⅝-in. crown molding. Because the mold-ing on the rake and the molding on the eave are in different planes, these two pieces can be dif-ficult to miter. In this case, the joint was compli-cated further because the bottom cove of the eave crown molding was ripped off where it meets the top of the 2x14 corona.

One way to improve the alignment of the rake and eave moldings is to use a 4⅝-in. crown on the rake and a 3½-in. crown on the eave. A more precise way is to have the crown molding for the eaves milled to a slightly different profile so that it matches the rake crown as the two pieces come together at the miter. This is the method the old-timers might have used, and on a bigger job we would have taken this approach. Instead, we adjusted the eave molding by tipping it down and away from the roof slightly and filing it so that the miter appears perfect to the eye.

Once the roof moldings were on and painted, we installed a rubber ice and water barrier over the plywood and over the edge of the crown molding, trimming it with a utility knife. We then stapled down 15-lb. felt paper and, over that, nailed a starter course of red-cedar shingles to serve as the drip edge. A cedar drip edge is slow-er to install than an aluminum one, but it looks much better on houses such as this one.

Curved collar ties frame the ceiling—Final-ly, on went the fiberglass shingles, step flashed with 6-in. by 8-in. pieces of copper that are bent

Saw kerfs define the dentils. The dentil molding was milled with a sliding miter saw set to cut almost through a pine trim board.

at right angles. We slipped the flashing behind the existing wall shingles after clipping the nails with a reciprocating saw. It was a relief finally to have a roof over our heads, if only in a man-ner of speaking.

Our plan for the portico called for a high, curved ceiling that left little room for collar ties. With a fairly flat roof pitch and no ties, we were concerned that the roof would spread over time. We solved the problem by designing curved col-lar ties that also would serve as backing for the curved ceiling (photo top right). One tie for each pair of rafters was made from 5/4x12 white pine. We could not get the entire curve from the

The portico was built to match existing conditions. The dimensions of the portico and the pitch of the portico's roof were determined largely by the width of the stoop and the height of the second-story window above.

Column profile used to lay out pilaster—By now the columns had arrived. They were cut to length and thoroughly primed according to the manufacturer's specifications. Column bottoms take a lot of wear and tear from the weather, so it's important to seal and install them properly. We applied a thick bead of polyurethane caulk to the top and bottom of each column before attaching the capitals and bases with screws. We like to use Sika LM polyurethane caulk (Sika Corp., 201 Polito Ave., Lyndhurst, N. J. 07071; 800-933-7452) at all crucial joints. It stays flexible, moves as wood expands and contracts, sticks tenaciously to almost anything and is paintable. Sheet-lead flashing was placed over the capital before the columns were put in place, plumbed and attached to the roof.

Earlier, before installing the columns, we used one column as a template to lay out the two flat pilasters below the portico at the house. The ancient Greeks knew that due to an optical illusion, a straight-edged column appears concave. They used entasis, a convex curving taper from bottom to top, to counteract this illusion. Correctly made columns should exhibit this gentle curve, which begins one-third of the way up on a Tuscan column.

We ripped, planed, caulked and screwed together the pine pilasters. They were held plumb against the shingles, and the curving line was marked out. As before, we cut through the shingles with a circular saw. The pilasters were nailed in place and caulked. We attached the trim here—and throughout the job—using a pneumatic trim gun and 8d galvanized nails.

A beaded ceiling follows the curve—Period porticoes usually had plastered or paneled wood ceilings. We opted for ½-in. by 4-in. beaded, tongue-and-groove fir wainscot. Available at most lumberyards, it's a quick, attractive solution that looks right on almost any porch. We nailed it up with an 18-ga. brad nailer and 1⅜-in. brads. A quarter-round molding covering the ends of the wainscoting completed the ceiling.

As a last detail, we decided to include modillion brackets running up the raking cornice. We chose a simple shape, known as a block modillion, as opposed to the complex molded brackets that the Greeks or the Romans would have carved. Each block, fabricated to sit plumb on the frieze, is trimmed at the soffit with ½-in. bed molding.

Finally, we patched in the sidewall shingles with red cedar to match the existing, caulked all the joints and painted the portico with two coats of gloss-white oil paint. ☐

Christopher Wuerth is a restoration contractor in Hamden, Connecticut. Photos by Reese Hamilton, except where noted.

12-in. boards, so we added pieces to the bottom of each rib.

With the roof firmly trussed, we were ready to turn our attention to the various boards and moldings that make up the entablature, including the architrave and frieze. We executed our design, loosely patterned after the profiles and proportions of the ancient Greeks and Romans, mostly with stock moldings. Profiles not readily available were made on site with a router table.

The molding that divides the architrave and the frieze is not only an architectural element but also a piece of trim that covers the joint between two boards.

Site-made dentil molding—Following the lead of porticoes on other houses in the neighborhood, we decided to add a dentil course along the bottom of the cornice (bottom photo, facing page). We made the dentil molding on site with a sliding saw. We started by reducing the thickness of a pine 1x2 to ½ in. Then we placed the stock flat on the saw table and set the blade so that it would cut nearly but not quite through the stock. The ⅛-in. saw kerfs are about ¾-in. apart.

The dentils were installed below a 1x3 with a ¼-in. round bead at the lower edge. The resulting dentil course was simple and fast to install.

Row-House Revision

Raising the floor level and digging out the backyard terrace brought light into the heart of this town house

by Charles Aquino

There is always a variety of impediments to re-designing a house and building an addition. In the case of this late-18th century, wood-framed Federal town house, the owners wanted more space and more light. But the impediments were a mandate not to alter the front facade, common walls shared with neighbors on both sides and a house that was already three-and-a-half stories tall. So we decided we could dig our way out of the problems.

The house is on a quiet street in Old Town Alexandria, Virginia. Unfortunately, the house had been remodeled crudely over the years, leaving few of the original details intact. The back of the house had been obscured by a 20th-century addition of little character.

The front door of the house is located in a small alcove about 4 ft. below the public sidewalk (bottom photo, p. 51). The entry leads into the basement level of the house, which included a windowless kitchen and a dining room that was equally dark. At the back of the house, the terrace was level with the dining-room ceiling. An exterior terrace that was surrounded by 6-ft. pri-

A lowered terrace brings light into a new room. In the photo on the facing page, taken at A on floor plan, the terrace was lowered to the floor level of the new family room, shown above. Photo taken at B on floor plan.

vacy walls on each side added to the dungeon-like feeling.

Formal and informal rooms—The owners wanted a light-filled home with both comfortable, informal living areas and more elegant areas for entertaining. They particularly wanted a formal dining room and an informal family room, both strongly connected to the kitchen (drawing facing page). They also wanted to improve the entry and to add additional storage space and bedrooms.

Both the owners and I agreed that the front rooms on each of the three upper floors (the formal living room and two bedrooms) would be restored to their original finishes, their character preserved. The final design for the project included a near total renovation of the rest of the existing interior and the construction of a new structure to the rear of the existing building. The new structure was designed to include a family room on the first floor with a master bedroom on the second (drawings below).

Construction difficulties—Originally, most of the houses on the block had side alleys that allowed access to the backyards. But subsequent infill houses had left the house I worked on landlocked on three sides. The only way to get to the backyard for the excavation work was through the house. This was done with a small Bobcat loader capable of moving through the 3-ft. masonry opening of the front door, through the basement and up a ramp (with minimum headroom). And to complicate matters further, the adjoining wall shared with the house on the east and the side garden walls required extensive underpinning before excavation for the planned addition could begin. The builders—PMA Master Builders of Alexandria, Virginia—were incredibly careful and patient with this difficult work, which laid the foundation for the ultimate success of the project.

Revamping the basement—Not surprisingly, the basement was a dark, unpleasant space with only very small amounts of indirect natural light reaching the front and rear rooms. The unavoidable lack of windows along the sides of the town house exacerbated the gloomy, subterranean feel of the space. I wanted to bring as much light into the basement as possible, and because, by necessity, the front door comes into the basement, I wanted to provide an entrance to the

SPECS

Bedrooms: 4
Bathrooms: 3½
Heating system: Gas-fired, forced hot air with A/C
Size: New construction: 777 sq. ft.
Cost: NA
Completed: 1992
Location: Alexandria, Virginia

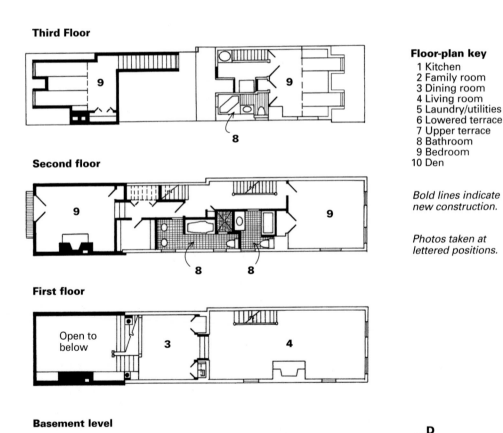

Floor-plan key
1 Kitchen
2 Family room
3 Dining room
4 Living room
5 Laundry/utilities
6 Lowered terrace
7 Upper terrace
8 Bathroom
9 Bedroom
10 Den

Bold lines indicate new construction.

Photos taken at lettered positions.

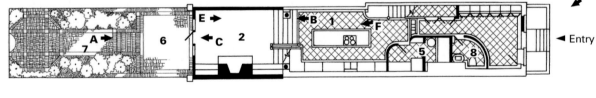

Four-level town house, 14 ft. wide. *The addition to the rear of the house added a family room with bedrooms above. A wide staircase from the family room to the kitchen brings light into the reconfigured basement level.*

Drawings: Jeff Bellantuono

An upper and lower terrace. The lowered terrace visually extends the feeling of spaciousness in the new family room. Photo taken at C on floor plan.

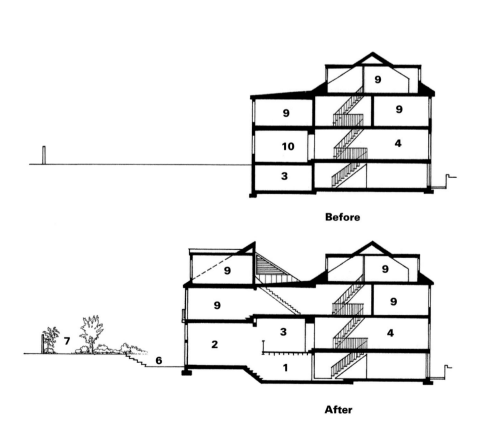

Before

After

Raise the floor, lower the terrace and add a three-story addition. *The house is hemmed in by neighbors on both sides and the sidewalk in front. Building onto the rear of the house was the only option.*

Historic-district town house. The local design-review board mandated that the front facade of the house could not be altered. The front door of the house is on the left, 4 ft. below the level of the sidewalk. Photo taken at D on floor plan.

Up six steps to the dining room, down six to the kitchen. The floor level of the new family room is between the two floors of the original house. The 12-ft. family-room ceiling is at the same height as the dining-room ceiling. An open railing adds to the spaciousness of the dining room. Photo taken at E on floor plan.

home that would be elegant as well as functional. The east side of the redesigned entry hall is lined with a row of raised-panel storage cabinets. Enclosed by a curving wall, a powder room and a laundry/utility room are placed against the west side of the space.

The curved walls of the entry are designed to permit light to move through the space and penetrate as deeply as possible into the interior of the basement. This helps to de-emphasize the feeling of being underground. If the house were larger or if there were more buildable space on the lot, a new addition could contain a new kitchen. But because of space constraints, the kitchen, a half-bath and the laundry room had to remain in the basement. The new kitchen, in the early 20th-century addition, lies just beyond the curving wall of cabinets. An open hallway runs from the entry hall to the kitchen.

A raised floor and a lowered terrace—The floor of the family room in the new addition is midway between the basement and first-floor level of the original house (drawing p. 51). At the transition between the old house and the new addition, a pair of stairways—one up to the dining room and one down to the kitchen—emcompasses the house's full 14-ft. width (drawing p. 50).

The ceiling of the family room is extended to a height of more than 12 ft., which, essentially, aligns the new ceiling with the ceilings of the

rooms on the first floor. The focus of the exterior wall of the family room is a pair of 8-ft. double French doors that have a fanlight above (photo p. 49). The full-height French doors and glazed fanlight both bring a great deal of light into the family room.

Originally, the ground level of the terrace outside the family room was about 4 ft. above the interior floor height. Lowering the terrace so that it is a half-step below the family-room floor height accomplished several things (photo p. 48). First, it meant that one no longer had to climb steps immediately upon going outside. Second, the lowered terrace height visually extends the space of the new family room (top photo, p. 51). Also, the terrace is visible from the kitchen below (photo below), further neutralizing the subterranean effect of the original basement. The light well created by the broad stair from the family room to the kitchen floods the kitchen with light.

In order to bring light and a feeling of spaciousness to the small formal dining area, the rear wall of the prior addition was removed on the first-floor level. A railing separates the dining room from the family room (photo left), and it also affords diners an unobstructed view of the terrace and garden. ☐

Charles Aquino is an architect in Richmond, Virginia. Photos by Andrew Lautman except where noted.

A subterranean kitchen. The kitchen has no windows of its own, but light comes into the room from the family room's French doors as well as from the front hall. Exposing the kitchen ceiling joists increased the feeling of height in the room and provided a recess for the incandescent lighting. Photo taken at F on floor plan.

A New Plan for an Old House

Instead of adding square footage to a mediocre house, the author revamped the floor plan and unified the exterior

by Dennis Wedlick

Redesigning a ranch. Prior to the author's renovation, the house was a series of outdated additions (bottom). It was subsequently transformed into a harmonious blend of flanking porches and sweeping gables (top). A V-shaped prow of six banked windows lets light into the living room. Photos taken at A on floor plan.

Often, it is tempting for owners to spend all their renovation money on additional square footage, contenting themselves with the as-is portion of their house simply because it already exists or because they have already spent money on it. But this job was different. I was able to convince my clients not to spend their money on enlarging their house. Instead, we agreed that the goal of this renovation should be to enhance the existing design—to create a cohesive, attractive exterior and improve the use and quality of the existing interior spaces.

The house is set on a hill flanked by carefully tended gardens. Prior to renovation, the house consisted of three combined structures (bottom photo, facing page). The oldest structure, a small farm shed, contained the kitchen. This was attached to the second-oldest structure, the garage. The largest and newest structure—a one-story ranch attached at the rear of the shed and the garage—contained the living room and the bedrooms. Recently, the garage had been enclosed for additional recreation space, and a shed dormer, which ran the full length of the ranch, had been added to the rear of the roof for additional bedrooms and a bath.

This hodgepodge of connected buildings was not only unattractive but also ill-conceived. The house did not have a proper entrance, an efficient kitchen, a dining room or enough windows for adequate light or views of the property.

Problems of the past—The construction that was done to the house over the past 40 years had simply provided more sheltered area. New rooms, windows and doors were added without considering how the combination of those elements would make for better living space.

Consequently, the house contained ample floor area to meet the owners' requirements, but its tortured floor plan made the house appear smaller than it was.

Because the kitchen entrance was located at the end of the drive, it served as the home's front door, forcing visitors to squeeze past the refrigerator when they came inside. And although efforts had been made to provide sufficient windows on the garden side of the house, the units installed only minimally accomplished the task and did not add to the home's appearance.

To make matters worse, the most recent expansion of the house was the epitome of thoughtless renovation. A massive shed dormer stuffed into the attic of the ranch portion of the house added two bedrooms with low ceilings and a bath. Spanning the full length of the house, the dormer left a mere 6 in. of roof at each end to define the shape of the gable. The dormer made the house look like a flat-roofed, two-story box with asphalt fringe. Fortunately, this side of the home sits at the bottom of a steep ridge, which allowed the bulk of the damage to go unnoticed.

Redesigning the house—Once we made the decision to work within the footprint of the existing house as much as possible, the next step was to determine the design direction and a theme by which the randomly assembled buildings could be visually unified and given an architectural character.

When the original ranch was added to the garage, its gable end was nearly centered over the added porch. This accidental composition became the theme for the exterior renovation. By adding gables and porches, the renovated house became a series of building layers, a collage of symmetrical and asymmetrical compositions (top photo, facing page).

Dormers that function as gables—I added two new gabled facades to the house—one on the entry side and one on the garden side. Although these facades appear to be substantial additions to the existing structure, they are not, in

Defining a doorway. A gable facade was centered over the doorway at the head of the driveway for a symmetrical look. The door had always been the house's most-used entry. Adding the facade and redesigning the floor plan changed the status of this entrance from ill-designed back door to elegant front door. The porch on the right extends the line of the original gable. Photo taken at B on floor plan.

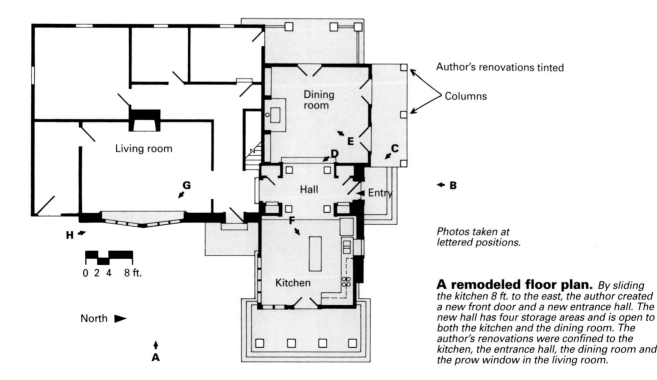

Living room

Dining room

Hall

Entry

Kitchen

Author's renovations tinted

Columns

Photos taken at lettered positions.

H

G

F

E

D

C

B

A

0 2 4 8 ft.

North ▶

A remodeled floor plan. *By sliding the kitchen 8 ft. to the east, the author created a new front door and a new entrance hall. The new hall has four storage areas and is open to both the kitchen and the dining room. The author's renovations were confined to the kitchen, the entrance hall, the dining room and the prow window in the living room.*

Trim and soffit. **A 1-ft. wide 5/4 pine band travels around the exterior of the house above the door and window heads. A urethaned pine soffit above the band further emphasizes the horizontal line. Photo taken at C on floor plan.**

Details inside and out. **The columns in the new hallway are identical, except for their clear finish, to the ones that border the porches. The new entry hall turns what was once the back door of the house into an elegant front entrance. Photo taken at D on floor plan.**

fact, additions to the footprint at all, and they required no structural foundation work. The top half of each facade is actually a dormer built over the existing roof, and the bottom half is merely a thickening of the existing wall (bottom photo, p. 58). Both gabled facades extend below the original eaves, further enhancing the illusion of layers.

The first and smallest gable was added to the former kitchen shed to create a proper entrance facade (photo p. 55). Even though it was known as the back door, the door at the top of the driveway was the entry used most often, so it needed special treatment. Centering the dormer over the door gives the entry a substantial, symmetrical look. Visitors to the house no longer find themselves in a quandary about which door to knock on when they come to the house. The back door has become, in effect, the front door.

The second and larger gable was added to the side of the former ranch, mimicking the gable over the new entrance. The second gable has six 6-ft. tall, double-hung windows that meet in the middle in an obtuse-angled prow (bottom photo, p. 58). These new larger windows replaced the bay window of the living room.

The trimwork for the new facades features a painted 1-ft. wide 5/4 pine band that tracks around the house at the heads of all windows and doors. Above the band is a urethaned pine soffit (photo left). The soffit enhances and further delineates the height of the windows, the

doors and the porches. Raised panels, which mimic exterior shutters, were added to the sides of some of the windows.

Porches—Two porches were added to the house, and two existing porches were renovated to match the new ones. The many porches with their different exposures not only provide for a variety of covered outdoor spaces, but they also contribute to the architectural theme of layered structures.

The porch added to the west side of the new dining room is the greatest improvement to the home's appearance. It is on this side of the house that the infamous shed dormer was most visible. The porch roof was designed to extend what remained of the old roofline of the former ranch, and as a result, the side of the shed dormer recedes into the background. Although this porch primarily faces the cliff side of the house, the additional covered space proves quite functional as a utility porch for wood storage and the like.

On the east side of the house, I added a porch off the kitchen (top photo, p. 54). This porch faces the lawn and the gardens, and it is a favorite place for sitting and drinking coffee on warm mornings.

Redirecting traffic—Beyond the front door a new entry hall (photo below) was created by sliding the kitchen 8 ft. to the east. This move required the only new foundation work for the

Wood shelves, woodstove. What started life as a garage was turned into a dining room. It is across the hall from the kitchen and can be used for formal dining as well as recreational activities. Photo taken at E on floor plan.

Sliding the kitchen 8 ft. Moving the kitchen 8 ft. to the east made room for the new entry hall (bottom photo, facing page). Kitchen stools can be slid under the island when they're not in use (above). Photo taken at F on floor plan.

entire renovation. The new entry hall leads directly to the existing living room and is completely open to the new kitchen to the east and a new dining room to the west. The hall is flanked by columns that are identical, except for their clear finish, to the ones that border the porches. The similar forms—both inside and out—help unify the house.

Before renovation, everyone entered the house through the kitchen. This was disruptive to the cook and inconvenient for the person who entered. Coats, boots and parcels all had to be carried through the kitchen and stored elsewhere. The new hall includes two closets, a boot box/ seat and a telephone nook with storage below.

Because the kitchen was no longer in the circulation path, it could be more efficiently laid out. The new kitchen has room for a breakfast table, an island and 25 ft. of cabinets and counter space (bottom photo, p. 57).

Across the hall from the kitchen, the dining room has built-in bookshelves and cabinets flanking an inglenook for a woodstove (top photo, p. 57). It works equally well for both formal dinners and recreational use.

The three spaces—entry, kitchen and dining room—act as a large hall when filled with guests, making the house ideal for parties. The spaces are open to each other and are surrounded by clusters of double-hung windows and French doors, enhancing the feel of spaciousness.

The prow—During preliminary discussions, the clients considered redoing the whole living room. But I was able to convince them that the addition of a large prow of windows would let much-needed light into the room and thus make it feel both larger and redone.

Built as an extension from the original floor, the prow window is only 18 in. deep (top photo, this page). To avoid having to match the existing floor at the prow's base, an extended sill fills the entire prow. This overscaled window seat changes the entire living room, drawing it into the garden and flooding it with light.

The cost of the renovation was substantial. And if one were to evaluate the investment on a cost-per-square-foot basis, it would seem foolishly extravagant. This, however, would be an improper assessment. Instead, the house must be evaluated on its comparative worth prior to and after the renovation. Furthermore, the time and the money were not spent by the owners merely for financial return. They wanted to create a home they could treasure as much as the landscaped parcel on which it is situated.

Improving the quality of a home's architecture, not just increasing its size, should be of prime importance to homeowners and their architects when considering a renovation project. In the case of the house shown here, previous renovations resulted in more space but not in quality architecture. To realize the full return on the investment of any renovation, the renovation needs to be the result of a carefully planned, aesthetically pleasing design. ☐

Dennis Wedlick is an architect in New York City. Photos by Jefferson Kolle except where noted.

Letting in light. **At first the clients considered redesigning their whole living room. The author convinced them that a tall, pointed bank of windows would give the room new character. Photo taken at G on floor plan.**

Dormers as gables. **The house's new gable ends are not, in fact, gables at all. The top half of each facade is actually a dormer built over the existing roof, and the bottom half is merely a thickening of the existing wall. Tall double-hung windows replaced the living room's bay window and afford views of the lawn and the gardens. Photo taken at H on floor plan.**

Row-House Renovation

Living amid the dust and the debris, urban owner-builders remove walls and add skylights to open up their inner-city house

by Robert Van Vranken

In the dark winter months of 1986, my wife, Jean, and I wrote checks for more money than we had ever seen before and moved into our first house—a small 1870 row house in Brooklyn, N. Y. (photo right). After 116 years the house was still standing with as much structural integrity and determination as the Brooklyn Bridge—also built around 1870. But like the bridge, successive improvement efforts had obscured the house's beauty.

Previous owners had covered old plaster with layer upon layer of drywall, added coats of paint to marble fireplaces and hung dropped ceilings that obscured plaster moldings. Even the one skylight in the house had been covered with paint.

In February, while sitting at our tiny kitchen table with all of the lights on at noon, we decided on a design strategy. Jean and I were operating on a very limited budget, so to save money, we planned to do most of the work ourselves. We would remove walls and dropped ceilings wherever possible, and we would add windows, skylights and glazed doors wherever we could. The tricky part would be integrating the 19th-century details into an open and airy floor plan, which included a new, larger bathroom and an updated kitchen.

Planning the attack—The house was a warren of small rooms: a kitchen and a living room on the first floor, two bedrooms on the second floor and a bath and two other small rooms on the top floor. Partition walls and long hallways made the house seem even smaller than its 1,500 sq. ft.

The house is only 14-ft. wide. Massive 3x12 joists, 12 in. o. c., run the width of the building. There were no load-bearing interior walls inside, so we were able to remove any and all interior partitions without jeopardizing the structural integrity of the house.

On the first floor, by removing the interior walls between the living room, the hall and the

All in a row. The author's house is in the center of the photo above. Because there is no front yard, construction debris from all three floors had to be stored in the living room until it could be hauled away (photo below). Careful planning and two years of sweat equity resulted in a low-cost renovation.

kitchen, we would transform the floor into one large room, divided only by the sweep of the open, curving staircase. Natural light from windows on the front and the back of the house would penetrate deep into the open, airy space.

The second floor was in much better shape than the first and third floors; stripping paint from the marble mantelpieces was all we needed to do. On the top floor we would install numerous skylights and enlarge the bathroom by removing an unneeded closet. Walls between the hall and the bedroom—the room I would later use as a studio—would be taken out, giving the same open effect we wanted on the first floor.

Living in the wreckage—Being young, strong and naive, I eagerly attacked the top floor. I was amazed by the amount of damage I did to our little house in no time at all. In less than a week I gutted the entire floor and carried all the debris—plaster, drywall, bathroom fixtures, decorative tin, tile, studs, whatever—one garbage can at a time, down three flights of stairs. By that time the house was in a fairly tragic state, so I went ahead with the planned demolition on the first floor as well. At one point, the living room, our dump pro tem, held 30 cu. yd. of debris (photo below), leaving us with only a small path to the front door. We eventually found someone who agreed to haul away the debris at a price we could afford

After the demolition was finished, I first added a window at the top of the stairs and installed four skylights in the roof. The roof leaked before I put in the skylights. After they were installed, the leaks were worse; I remember lying in bed early one Sunday morning during a torrential downpour, listening to joint-compound buckets fill with water at a rate that made sleep impossible. Eventually I had to reroof the whole building.

Once the skylights were installed, the top floor became the bright spot of the house; now

I could finally see what I was working on (top left photo, facing page).

Bigger, brighter bathroom—The bathroom was next. Jean and I wanted a large shower—more like a walk-in shower room—but we didn't want a door separating the room from the rest of the bathroom. We built a glass-block wall, which affords a little privacy and keeps in the water. A skylight over the shower and the glass-block wall allow natural light to flood the whole bathroom. Although a simple prefab shower stall would have been easier and cheaper to install, the shower room turned out to be a real success. It is one of the most notable features of the house.

We built the cabinets and the countertop into the space previously occupied by a closet. Then a tilesetter tiled the bathroom in a beautiful combination of white and cobalt blue (photo below).

One afternoon when I needed a break from construction, I took a stroll outside. While walking, I found a huge 5/16-in. beveled-edge mirror leaning against a bunch of trash cans. It was perfect for our new bathroom.

After attacking the entire top floor head-on, Jean and I were completely overwhelmed. A full-scale assault on your house is also a full-scale assault on your life.

For two months, all during the dirty demolition work and subsequent rebuilding, we had been bathing in a grungy stall shower in the basement. When the new bathroom was finished, taking a shower amid the sparkling tile and shiny glass block was a special treat.

Rejuvenating the staircase—The house's curving three-story staircase is perhaps the primary architectural feature, but it was in rough shape. The steps squeaked loudly, and most of the treads were worn and split. I numbered the stair pieces according to a diagram and then removed newel posts, balusters, handrails, treads and risers. I sanded down the risers and replaced the treads with 5/4 yellow pine.

Restoring the balustrade was an arduous chore, which involved several rounds of paint stripper, some scraping and a lot of sanding. After reassembling the stairs, we painted them. As an experiment I stained the treads but painted the tread returns white, and I was surprisingly pleased with the results (top right photo, facing page). Finally, the path to the finished bathroom on the third floor—our oasis from the dust and the debris—was complete.

New kitchen, old components—Jean and I knew that being without a kitchen was going to be a major inconvenience, so we prepared as thoroughly as possible. We bought the appliances and all the building materials beforehand and stored them in the living room. The idea was not to waste a lot of time battling Brooklyn traffic going to and from the lumberyard. We signed up a good friend to help out with several days of cabinet building. We were able to leave the sink and the stove hooked up until the new ones were ready to go in. Before we started on the cabinetry, I replaced the door to the backyard with a divided-lite glazed door. With the extra light now

pouring into the kitchen, the room's dreariness factor was immediately cut in half.

For the countertops we used some beautiful, old, 7/8-in. thick marble from a store that sold used architectural elements. For $40 apiece we bought 2½-ft. by 6-ft. slabs, which were very smooth but chipped, stained and weathered wonderfully. We cut the slabs ourselves, using a masonry blade on a standard 8¼-in. circular saw. It was very slow going; we could only cut a 1/8-in. deep kerf with each pass of the saw, but this method did work.

The slabs were simply set into place, and they haven't budged. I have seen other countertops made of pristine, highly polished marble, but I prefer the romance of our old, imperfect slabs. For any chef, marble is a wonderful surface to work on, and the slabs attract the attention of all our guests (bottom photo, facing page).

The results—After living in our finished house for about a year, we declared the project a success. The total cost of the project came to $27,525, roughly $23 per sq. ft. In a city where renovation costs can range from $75 to $125 per

sq. ft., the advantage of providing our own labor is immediately apparent.

But most importantly, the house is no longer a dark and creepy place. The large terrace door, the skylights and the new window (a total addition of only 37 sq. ft. of glass) have added a remarkable amount of light and significantly changed the feeling of the entire house.

The new, more-open floor plan does several things. First, it alleviates the oppressive sense of boxy claustrophobia. Second, it helps distribute natural light evenly through the interior. Third, the house is now full of interesting perspectives; there are longer views of the interior that are appealing in their own right but also add an impression that the house is longer than it actually is. And finally, the mix of old and new architectural features—pine floors, plaster moldings, marble slabs—in conjunction with skylights and modern kitchen and bath equipment—gives the house a unique character that makes it a comfortable and inviting place. □

Robert Van Vranken is a fine-arts painter who now lives in Brunswick, Maine. Photos by the author.

Glass blocks and shiny tiles. Finishing the bathroom first gave the owners a clean oasis amid the dirty job site. The huge bevel-edge mirror was found on the street by the author.

Revamped staircase. Replacing split treads, stripping paint from the balustrade and painting the tread returns restored the stairs to their former glory (photo above).

Let there be light. The addition of a skylight and a window at the top of the stairs brought much-needed light all the way down to the first floor (photo left).

Opening up the kitchen. Open shelves and a glazed door to the backyard deck give the kitchen a bright, airy feel (photo below). Salvaged marble slabs cover the counters.

Rock-Bottom Remodel

How an architect turned an old garage into his house and office

by Ira Kurlander

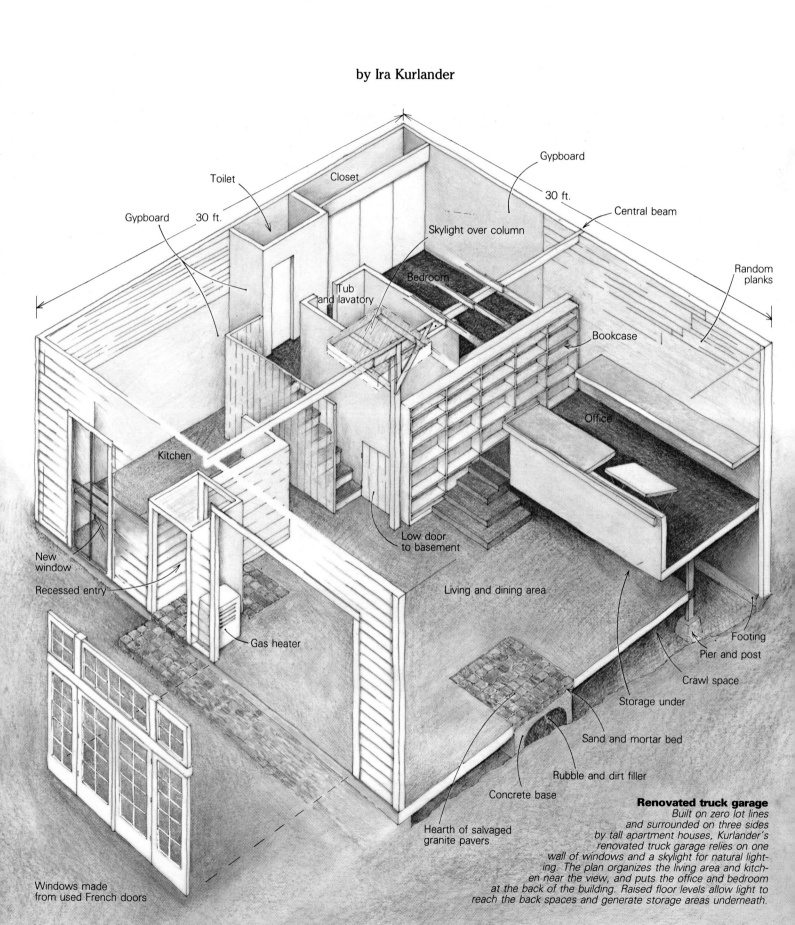

Gypboard

Gypboard

30 ft.

Toilet

Closet

30 ft.

Central beam

Skylight over column

Random planks

Tub and lavatory

Bedroom

Bookcase

Office

Kitchen

Low door to basement

New window

Recessed entry

Living and dining area

Footing

Pier and post

Gas heater

Crawl space

Storage under

Sand and mortar bed

Rubble and dirt filler

Concrete base

Hearth of salvaged granite pavers

Renovated truck garage
Built on zero lot lines and surrounded on three sides by tall apartment houses, Kurlander's renovated truck garage relies on one wall of windows and a skylight for natural lighting. The plan organizes the living area and kitchen near the view, and puts the office and bedroom at the back of the building. Raised floor levels allow light to reach the back spaces and generate storage areas underneath.

Windows made from used French doors

Sometimes the most challenging design problems an architect gets are those with the most limitations. I'd purchased a piece of inner-city property with a 900-sq. ft. outbuilding at the back of the lot, and wanted to convert it into my office and residence, so that I could rent out the main house to help pay the mortgage. But this old truck garage, built in the 1920s, had an uncommon set of restrictions that I'd have to design around.

Three of the four 30-ft. long walls of the building were located on property lines, and the law required them to remain windowless. Inside, the 13-ft. ceiling was too low to allow a second floor, and a column occupied the exact center of the building. To make matters worse, the garage had already been converted into a dingy, poorly organized dwelling. Last, local codes and my $7,000 budget meant that I wouldn't be able to increase the size of the building. My only alternative was to rearrange the interior spaces.

A multi-level floor plan—I gutted the building, and while I sorted and stacked the reusable materials, I pondered my options. Given a choice, people will move toward the part of a room that offers natural light and an outdoor view. I could put windows only on the south wall, so I located the living and dining area and the kitchen in that sunny part of the building (drawing, facing page).

Taking advantage of the fact that the low-pitch shed roof was highest to the north, I arranged the interior like a theater, with rooms far from the windows lifted above the main floor to get an unobstructed view and more light. The office is 30 in. higher than the living area, separated from it by a low wall that defines the space and provides a needed measure of privacy. In plan, the office may seem isolated, but the view of the garden from the drafting table makes this workspace seem larger, and more a part of the rest of the house.

I placed the bedroom in the darkest corner at the highest possible level (60 in. above the main floor). For convenience, I located the bathroom on the same level. I built some badly needed storage space into the area between the slab and the bedroom floor, reducing the number of head-bumping joists by spanning the widely spaced 4x6 beams with extra-strong 2½-in. tongue-and-groove decking. Someday, the washer and drier will be located in this generous storage area. If I could get a window into it, I would be tempted to convert it to a second bedroom.

The only walls in the house that actually

Three pairs of recycled French doors fit together to fill the original garage-door opening. Waxed hardboard floors in the living and dining area, above right, are inexpensive and easy to clean; they give a pleasant earth-tone background to the area rugs and cobblestone hearth.

A broad cobblestone step, right, sweeps across the courtyard and links the garden to the doorway. The recessed entry offers shelter, and makes the interior of the small house seem spacious by contrast.

reach the ceiling enclose the toilet. The other rooms are open, and share light and ventilation, yet they remain clearly separate from one another. From the living area, it is impossible to see the mess in any of the other rooms, and the whole house can be tidied up quickly for clients or guests.

Because the local zoning code prohibits outside additions, I wasn't able to extend a typical roof projection over the front porch. Instead, I recessed an entry into the building, creating a sheltered area where I could fumble for my key while holding a bag of groceries. Because of the entry's small size (3 ft. square and 6 ft. 10 in. high), the interior of the house seems generous and expansive when you open the door. In fact, the space inside is larger than the courtyard, and the bottleneck entry makes the contrast still greater.

Windows for the south wall—The old double-door garage opening was about 12 ft. wide by 10 ft. high. I wanted to fill this space entirely with windows. Since a two-story building was located only 22 ft. to the south, the more height the windows had, the more sunlight they would let in. My first thought was to install a gas-station garage door with glass panels, but it was impossible to find one—at least one I could afford.

Instead, I decided to use French doors that I had collected from various remodelings. I combined three pairs, all of different widths, to create a low-budget window wall. The final arrangement (top photo, previous page) has a Palladian formality.

The framing for the new window was simple—4x4 posts from subfloor to header, with the two widest doors hung in the middle. I fixed the midsized pair in place on either side of the operable doors and ran the narrowest pair across the top. One full door was mounted sideways over the two center doors, and the last door was cut in half to fill the remaining gaps. For the time needed to replace a few broken panes plus the cost of the posts and trim, I had 120 sq. ft. of glass.

I needed an operable window with maximum ventilation for the kitchen. I took the easy way out and had a new aluminum casement made. It's the same height as the living-room window and runs all the way to the floor (photo facing page), thus opening the small kitchen to the garden outside.

The skylight—The lack of windows in the house tempted me to pepper the roof with skylights. But it's been my experience that lots of skylights with just a few windows is not a good combination; the skylights emphasize the lack of a view and suggest the feeling of being at the bottom of a well.

I decided to get by with a single skylight, placed right over the center column. Its location in the center of the house anchors the rambling collection of levels around the post, and transforms this obstacle into a unifying element. The skylight also helps to balance the light that comes in from the one window wall. One-quarter of the skylight is directly over the bathtub, giving this interior room a glimpse of the sky and the tall trees in the courtyard.

The 2-ft. o.c. roof joists favored a dome skylight either 4-ft. or 8-ft. square. I chose an economical 4-ft. square double-dome, and during noisy rainstorms and in cold weather, I am glad to have less skylight and more solid roof. Only one problem remains—the neighborhood raccoons have discovered that the skylight is a warm place to congregate.

Interior finishes—The original roof beam and joists are barely adequate for their spans, and 50 years had resulted in visible deflection. I chose to leave these members exposed, since covering them would have added considerable weight to the structure and cost a lot of money to boot. To strengthen and match the existing framing, I added roughsawn knee braces at the central post. Two of the interior walls were then partially sheathed with random-size planks salvaged from neighborhood debris bins. Fitting the various lengths and widths was time-consuming, and the many small cracks had to be caulked. But the only costs were for nails, caulk and the frequent saw sharpenings necessitated by cutting nail-embedded boards. These boards looked shabby at first, but when they were painted white, things came together. Work like this is best done by an amateur—I think it would drive a good carpenter crazy.

As an inexpensive substitute for a hardwood floor, I glued 4x8 sheets of $\frac{1}{4}$-in. tempered hardboard to the $\frac{3}{4}$-in. plywood underlayment. When it is machine waxed, this material's dark brown color acquires a depth and sheen that make a pleasing background for furniture and rugs. Unfortunately, the floor's location just off the courtyard garden means that lots of outdoor grit gets ground into the finish, and the hardboard needs power waxing and polishing three times a year to maintain its looks. Next time, I'll try a urethane-type coating as a sealant before waxing, for greater protection against moisture and scuffing.

The entry area and the hearth required a sturdier floor. Luckily (for me), streets in San Francisco's old produce market were being torn up, and the original granite cobblestone pavers were free to those who'd haul them away. I laid them on their sides in a bed of dry sand mixed with cement, so that they could be pushed around and leveled as needed. When the arrangement was satisfactory and the dry mortar joints were at an even height (about 1 in. below the top of the pavers), I topped off the mortar joints with sand and poured water over the surface. The sand kept the mortar mix from splashing, and retained moisture while the grout joints cured. After a week, I swept off the stones and vacuumed the loose sand out. Surprisingly, installing the pavers was the easiest part of the remodel. Later I added more pavers to the courtyard, making a broad step across the front of the house that includes both the French doors and the entry (bottom photo, previous page). Big design gestures like this make a small place feel larger.

A top-loading cast-iron stove from the 1890s helps heat the house and brightens up a windowless wall. Steps beside the bookcase-wall lead to the office, which has been left open to take advantage of the view, natural light and ventilation.

As seen from the top of the bedroom stairs, a custom casement window opens the kitchen to the garden and lets in fresh air. Second-hand cabinets and appliances behind the kitchen wall are in keeping with the white-washed paneling and sideboard, both made from salvaged planks.

The heating system—Since so few of the walls in the whole place reach the ceiling, an old freestanding gas heater is adequate for heating most of the house. An 1890s cast-iron stove (photo facing page) is the one thing I splurged on. Its Victorian decoration has great style, and although it's not airtight, it's still quite efficient. Its top-loading door, originally meant for coal, is handy for loading short lengths of wood and is neater than side-door designs that drop ashes on the hearth. And its mica windows let the firelight shine through.

Electrical—The entire electrical system was redone from scratch by a licensed electrician. To save his time (and my money), I had him run the wiring in exposed conduit and boxes along baseboards and beams. Later on I added a plug-in light track to the living-area ceiling for more lighting flexibility.

I like this exposed system, but if I'd had more time and money, I would have made custom metal cover plates to hide the punch-out sides of the electrical boxes. The present combination of plastic cover plates on metal switch boxes is unappealing.

Summing up—My only real regret is that I didn't install enough insulation. Next time I re-roof, I'll add a couple of inches of rigid foam on top of the 1-in. rigid fiberglass already installed, and when the time comes to renew the exterior siding, the walls will get a full 3½ in. of fiberglass batts.

The two most important lessons I learned from remodeling the garage were about economy and planning. Rather than diminishing the finished product, the strict budget made me search out alternative materials, which in turn set the style of the house. Having a flexible approach, I was able to switch from high-tech gas-station doors to traditional French doors. Instead of buying a sideboard for the dining area, I built one out of the same salvaged planks I used on the walls.

Hiding the kitchen behind a storage wall let me use an odd assortment of castoff kitchen cabinets. Likewise, the exposed roof joists and the view through the skylight make the old pedestal sink in the bath seem less obtrusive. I also avoided getting bogged down in hiding vents and flues. As long as the space is open and interesting, used materials and simple solutions to mechanical problems aren't distracting.

The open plan has indeed become a cliche of contemporary architecture, but sometimes it does make sense. This house has the same square footage as a four-room Victorian cottage that I used to live in. But even though the cottage had lots of windows and a good view, its hallways and boxy plan made it a tight maze compared to my transformed garage.

Trying for maximum light and openness within such demanding restrictions created pleasant, livable spaces, which I think is the ultimate goal of good architecture. □

Architect Ira Kurlander practices in San Francisco, Calif.

California Craftsman Remodel

Arts-and-Crafts details unify a 1950s ranch house and two outbuildings

A ranch house reborn. Although the author had originally intended to bulldoze this 1950s ranch house and its outbuildings to make way for a new spec house, she and her partner reconsidered. They extensively remodeled and added to the existing house instead. Photo taken at A on floor plan.

by Susan N. Smith

A few years ago my partner and I worked for months on plans for a Mediterranean-style spec house in Montecito, California. Eventually, we had everything we needed: plans, permits and a good lot. The 1950s ranch house and a few outbuildings on the property could be cleared out of the way. Then, at the last minute, our project took a turn that neither of us would have predicted.

Slowed down by the recession, the real-estate market had come to a near standstill. Lots of big, Mediterranean-style houses were just sitting on the market. Our spec-house plans began to look all wrong. The project looked so risky, in fact, that we decided to walk away from the $60,000 we had already invested and take a harder look at the house and outbuildings on the one-acre lot. We wondered whether a fresh approach to the project would show us a way to salvage the buildings. This change in strategy sent us looking for a different architectural style.

We found what we liked in the work of Bernard Maybeck, the Greene brothers and Gustav Stickley. Their Craftsman-style houses, inspired by the English Arts-and-Crafts movement and built in the early 1900s, are unified inside by carefully planned and detailed woodwork. Outside, broad roof pitches and timber trellises help these houses blend with the landscape. The style seemed much more in the spirit of the property we had bought. There was even a 1916 Maybeck just down the road to inspire us.

Because our company typically buys, remodels and resells houses, we realized that it made a lot more sense to enlarge the ranch house we originally intended to bulldoze. We hired architect Andy Neumann, then with Seaside Union Architects, to help us redirect the project. He showed us how to unify the buildings on the property. Another factor that contributed to the project's success was the craftsmanship of Tom Jackson and Frank Louda of Chismahoo Construction. Their woodworking talents and sense of design helped us sort out details as we went along.

The existing structures included the 1,600-sq. ft. main house, a garage that had been turned into a guest house and another small guest house. We didn't tear any of them down. Instead, we incorporated the garage and the guest house into the original house (drawings facing page) and used Craftsman-style details such as custom doors and trim to tie old and new parts of the house together. Over the first-floor bedroom and the family room, we added a second-floor guest bedroom and bathroom with adjoining deck. And finally, we built a master-bedroom wing (photo facing page).

We were our own clients, so we were free to pursue modifications. And we learned our biggest lesson at the start: Even though we had invested a lot of money in plans we didn't use, we discovered no situation is irretrievable. In the end, our about-face was the right choice.

Connecting the outbuildings—It took a lot of careful planning to link the house with the garage and the guest house. All three of these structures had been built on concrete slabs but at different elevations. We didn't need to change the height of the garage floor because it didn't matter that someone would have to take a few steps down to the garage. But the guest house, which we intended to turn into a new bedroom, was a different story: Its slab was lower than that of the main house, and we wanted finish floors on the first floor to be at the same height when the project was complete. To raise the height of the floor, the builders installed wooden sleepers over the existing slab, topped them with a plywood subfloor and put down carpet over that. The connecting space between the guest house and the main house was an open garden area, so we poured a slab there for a new family room at the same elevation as the main-house floor. These measures resulted in a first floor with a uniform elevation.

There also was the question of structural stability. The concrete slabs under the existing buildings were supported on the perimeter by footings about 1 ft. thick. The structural engineer on the project, however, thought that would be inadequate to support the added weight of the new second-floor guest room, bath and deck, and the weight of the new roof between the garage and the house. To increase the bearing

Photo facing page: Susan N. Smith   Drawings: Gary Williamson

Second floor

Guest room

Deck

North ▲

From unconnected components

The author unified an existing ranch house and two outbuildings, then added a new master-bedroom wing and a second-floor guest room. The master bedroom is 5½ ft. higher in elevation than the main floor, with the new guest room 4½ ft. above the master bedroom. The photo below shows the new family room under construction.

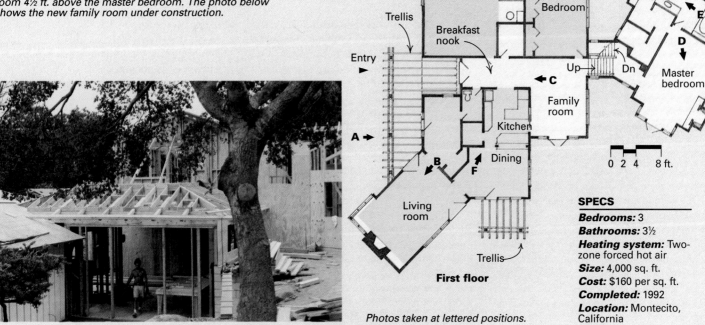

Original house and outbuildings shaded

Garage

Bedroom

Dressing area

Trellis

Breakfast nook

Entry ▲

Up

Dn

E ◀

D ↓

Master bedroom

A →

C ◀

Family room

Kitchen

B ↙

F ↖

Dining

Living room

0 2 4   8 ft.

Trellis

First floor

SPECS

Bedrooms: 3
Bathrooms: 3½
Heating system: Two-zone forced hot air
Size: 4,000 sq. ft.
Cost: $160 per sq. ft.
Completed: 1992
Location: Montecito, California

Photos taken at lettered positions.

capacity, we undermined edges of the slabs, drilled into the concrete to set dowels of ½-in. rebar and then poured new perimeter footings about 18 in. deep.

A house that towered over its site wouldn't have been compatible with its neighbors, so we decided to keep the rebuilt house low (photo p. 66). The new master-bedroom wing, which includes its own bath and dressing room, is 5½ ft. higher in elevation than the main floor of the house; a new second-floor guest room and attached deck is another 4½ ft. higher than that.

A key problem that Neumann helped us overcome was how to link the detached garage and the guest building behind the house smoothly. In addition to creating a new family room, we decided to turn the 7½-ft. space between the main house and the garage into a lofted hall with a breakfast nook at one end and skylights above (photo facing page). While this space helped tie the house together, it had to be tall enough to provide proper drainage for various intersecting roof planes. So that this area wouldn't overwhelm the rest of the house, we reduced the scale of the ceiling with trusses that alternate with skylights to create a light, airy feeling. The breakfast nook has its own entry to a trellised porch at the front of the house (photo p. 66).

In addition to some natural site restrictions, there was the ever-present fear of fire. A 1990 fire in Santa Barbara destroyed 530 houses and prompted much tougher fire codes, which we had to meet. One of them was a restriction on the size of timbers used outside, limiting them to a minimum of 6x6 (the theory is that they won't burn as readily as smaller material). We were permitted to use small timbers but only as long as we applied a special exterior paint that protects trim and timbers from burning when they're exposed to high heat. We had a lot of problems with the paint, though, and wouldn't recommend its use if it can be avoided. Other fire-code requirements were the use of ⅝-in. Type-X gypsum board beneath the siding and double-glazed windows. Type-X gypsum board uses chemical additives and glass fibers to help it resist heat, and double-glazed windows were viewed as a way of slowing down a fire's entry into a house. The windows alone added $30,000 to the project budget.

Unifying the parts—Our response to the steep grade of the property was a house shape that incorporates several different rooflines. We combined gable and hip roofs to link the existing building with the new family room, the bedroom wing and the second-floor space. This posed drainage as well as aesthetic difficulties, which took some thinking to resolve. A careful roof-drainage plan, which could also handle runoff from the second-floor deck, was essential. And because some rooflines were visible from both inside and outside the house, we took some care in choosing the right roofing material. We settled on Hardishake, a fireproof, cement-based material made to look like slate (James Hardie Building Products, Inc., 10901 Elm Ave., Fontana, Calif. 92335; 909-356-6300). We made the shingles look old by using two shades of gray and by breaking

Old room, new look. Once dark and oppressive with a low-ceiling (below), the living room in the original house is now light and airy (above). A wash coat of white on the ceiling allows most of the wood grain to show. The floor slate is laid in a herringbone pattern through the living room, the entry hall and the dining room. Photo taken at B on floor plan.

some of the corners to create an irregular pattern. A low cupola, capped by the Hardishakes, hides roof vents.

Originally, the house had been finished with redwood board-and-batten siding. We re-sided the house with clapboards, but we found a way to reuse the old redwood siding by removing it from the house and having it remilled. It was then used as trim inside and outside. The new beveled redwood siding is enhanced by detailing like beaded corner boards and window trim, and by decorative brackets beneath bow windows. Beams, trusses and corbels used in exterior trellises were individually detailed, with much of the inspiration coming from books on the work of Craftsman architects.

Redesigning interior spaces—Dark, choppy and unappealing when we found it, the main house had to be gutted. Ceilings were very low and oppressive, so in key areas like the living room (photos above), the hall and the breakfast room, we made ceilings higher. Cathedral ceilings with timbered roof trusses over the living

room and the hall off the kitchen (photo p. 71) help open those spaces, and skylights fill them with sunshine.

In the living room, the existing corner window was replaced by a Craftsman-style window incorporating small divided lites at the top of the frame and a large, single piece of glass below—a Craftsman trademark. When we tore out the ceiling in the living room, we found that the stone fireplace ended at ceiling height and looked awkward in a room that was now capped by a cathedral ceiling. We lowered the fireplace by tearing out some of the stonework and adding trim above. A thorough cleaning of the stone worked wonders.

Another interior challenge was that rooms abutted each other at angles other than 90°—a feature of the original floor plan. We used a slate floor in the entry, the dining room and the living room and set the tiles in a herringbone pattern, which eliminated the awkward transitions that would have resulted from setting floor tiles square to the walls. The finishing touch was the soft colors of the interior walls, which were inspired by the tan and rose colors in the stone, the slate and the wood.

Craftsman-inspired trim—The living room, the dining room and the entry together make up a large area—with different ceiling heights throughout. These rooms in particular needed to be unified, and to do that we used trim, casework, doors and windows modeled on Craftsman houses we had studied. To me, the style is simple, functional and direct. Except in some very expensive Craftsman houses, trim was rarely elaborate in the way that Victorian or even Colonial trim could be. And it is this detailing that is one of the most memorable features of houses built in the Craftsman style. The trim is a reflection of the 1990s as it is painted white; the traditional Craftsman treatment was to leave the trim the natural color of the wood.

Wainscoting in the entry and the dining room is medium-density fiberboard (MDF) capped with some of the original redwood board-and-batten siding that had been remilled. In the living room, we put this technique to work below the built-in window seat and on the wall above the fireplace. The kitchen, the breakfast room and the family room were unified with a continuous wainscoting throughout.

All of the interior doors were custom built from a Stickley drawing (top right photo, p. 70). A narrow, horizontal panel runs the width of the door on top; below are tall, narrow panels. In rooms where more light was needed, panes of glass, cut in small squares, were substituted for the top panel. Stickley originally was a cabinetmaker who went on to publish a variety of Craftsman-era house plans.

The kitchen cabinets also were custom-made and used door panels similar in style to the wainscoting used elsewhere in the house. We chose tile counters to set off the moldings and add a little zip to traditionally dull Craftsman kitchens. The bedrooms and the baths in the house reflect the same mix of contemporary and Craftsman styles. The ceilings in the master bedroom (top

Linking old and new. Brightened by skylights and a high, timbered ceiling, this breakfast nook replaced the narrow, 7½-ft. alley between the original house and the garage. The wainscoting is MDF; battens were milled from the original redwood siding. Photo taken at C on floor plan.

Easy access outside. The master-bedroom wing opens to a small grass terrace outside with access to the pool and the main house below or to an office off to the left. The stairs leading from the main floor to the master-bedroom suite rise a total of 5½ ft. Photo taken at D on floor plan.

Copied from Stickley. An epoxy-coated door to the shower in the master bathroom is patterned after those made by Gustav Stickley.

Craftsman-inspired windows. Windows in Craftsman-era houses often used patterns of square lites in different sizes, like this set of casement windows in the master bathroom. The ceiling was left high and open in the dressing-bath areas to unify these spaces. Photo taken at E on floor plan.

Let the light in. Skylights in the gallery next to the kitchen bring plenty of natural light inside. The kitchen cabinets were custom-made and used door panels similar in style to the wainscoting used elsewhere in the house. Tile countertops add some zip to the kitchen. Photo taken at F on floor plan.

left photo, facing page) and in the upstairs guest bedroom, for example, repeat the ceiling-truss theme and finish details used in the living room. A pattern of small squares, a common Craftsman detail in windows and trim, is used extensively throughout the house and is repeated in the master-bedroom mantel. The mantel is finished in tumbled marble (tumbled marble has been treated to make it look rough and old) that picks up the warm, brownish-pink of the walls.

The ceiling in the master bath (bottom photo, facing page) was made high and left open in the dressing-bath areas to unify the two spaces. But the toilet, shower and drying areas have lowered ceilings to provide intimacy and warmth. The shower door is unusual; it is also made in the Stickley style and painted with marine epoxy paint (top right photo, facing page).

A smooth landing—One of our final challenges was to work around a mother bird and her babies who were nesting in an air duct in the ceiling. At one point during construction, we had gently moved the nest outside and put it on a trellis where it would be out of harm's way. The bird responded by dive-bombing everyone on the site. So we gave up and moved the young family back to the air duct. This posed a prob-

lem as we tried to clean up the last details and get the house ready for sale. But the day before the opening of the house for friends and real-estate brokers, the birds repaid our kindness by flying off on their own, which left us just enough time to install the air duct's grill and finish the project. We sold the house six months after it was completed. Some of the big Mediterranean-style houses that were built at about the same time are still on the market. □

Susan N. Smith and partner Ernst A. Benzien run Homeworks Associates in Santa Barbara, Calif. Photos by Scott Gibson except where noted.

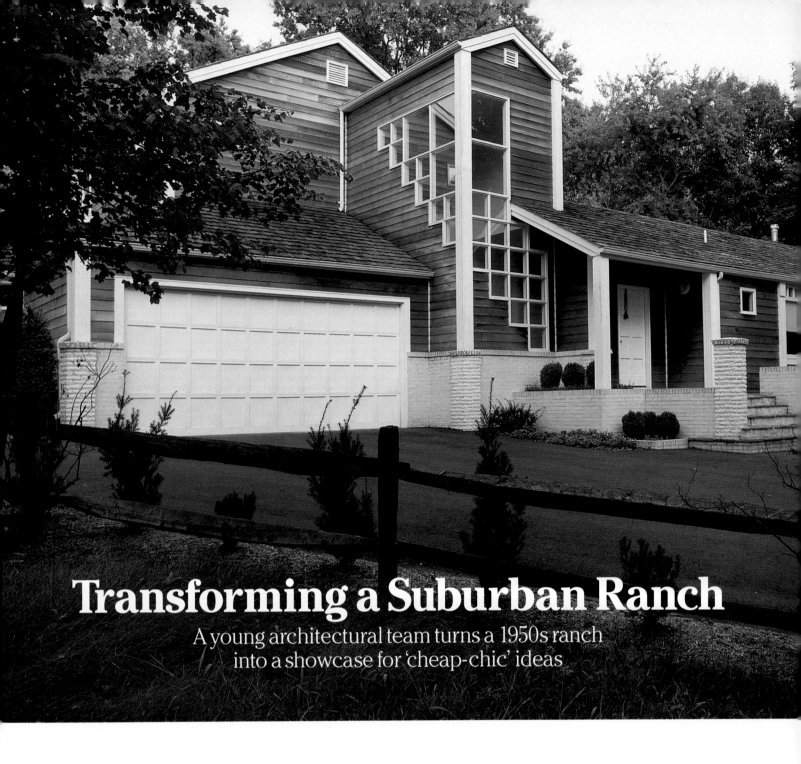

Transforming a Suburban Ranch

A young architectural team turns a 1950s ranch into a showcase for 'cheap-chic' ideas

by Jack Wilbern

In the 1930s, the Old Dominion Trolley Company ran its lines into McLean, Virginia, and after the track was abandoned some years later, the right-of-way became the main street that now bears the company's name. The trolley line and then the street made it easier for commuters to reach the District of Columbia, just eight miles away. And the huge post-war housing boom resulted in the construction of thousands of simple, affordable homes. Old farms that once dominated the area were gradually pushed aside. The suburbs had arrived.

The neighborhood matured over the following 40 years and is now considered a highly desirable place to live in the Washington area. It is not far from a city dominated by young, upper-income families. The appeal of the neighborhood

was why, several years ago, my partner, Sam Butz, and I found ourselves inspecting a dull, termite-ridden ranch with a For Sale sign out front (photo below right).

The house also looked like it might solve two problems we had at the time. Sam's family of four needed a house, and our newly formed architectural firm needed a tangible way of showing potential clients that we were capable of imaginative work. As dull as it was, the house was an opportunity, and we bought it.

We landed a mortgage that covered 95% of the cost of the 800-sq. ft. house, allowing us to save our cash for a major renovation. The house was a typical post-World War II ranch, an ultimate fixer-upper, but it did provide a partial foundation and a first-floor deck for the new building. And the

half-acre lot already had access to sewer, water, gas and electricity.

The addition we built was more than three times the size of the existing house. We added a kitchen and a family room to the back, with bedrooms and a deck above it, and we tied the old and new sections of the house together with a new dining room and an adjacent living room. We also built terraces in the back to improve access to the backyard.

Plans to save money—We started our nine-month project with champagne tastes and a beer budget. But we hoped that with careful planning and plenty of on-site ingenuity (a nice way of saying there would be too many architects on the job), we could do it without going broke. Our

Bottom photo, facing page: Jack Wilbern

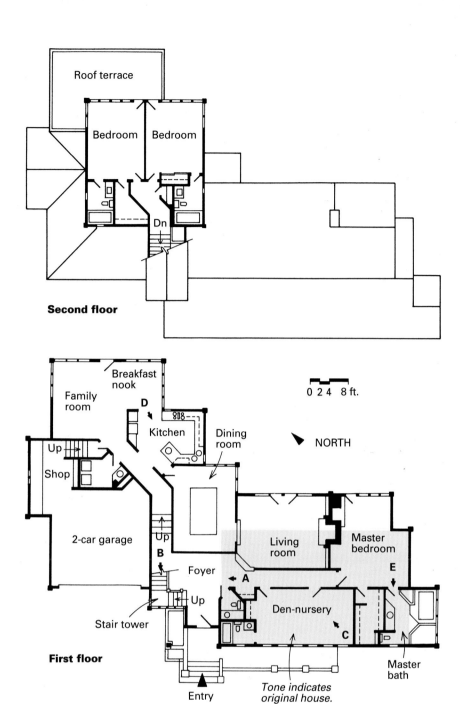

Roof terrace

Bedroom   Bedroom

Dn

Second floor

0 2 4 8 ft.

Family
room

Breakfast
nook

D

Kitchen

Dining
room

NORTH

Up

Shop

Living
room

Master
bedroom

2-car garage

Up

B

E

Foyer

A

Den-nursery

Up

Stair tower

C

First floor

Master
bath

Entry

*Tone indicates
original house.*

*A **new shape in front.** The rebuilt house (top photo) bears little resemblance to the 800-sq. ft. ranch the author and his partner bought (photo above). What remains of the original structure is to the right of the front door in the top photo.*

Expansion to the rear
The 2,600-sq. ft. addition is far bigger than the 800-sq. ft. ranch house the author and his partner bought. The nursery at the front of the house is part of the original structure. The new living areas were built to the rear of the house, away from the busy street in front.

SPECS

Bedrooms: *4*
Bathrooms: *4½*
Heating system: *Hybrid hot air, gas and electric heat pump*
Size: *3,400 sq. ft.*
Cost: *$88 per sq. ft.*
Completed: *1990*
Location: *McLean, Va.*

Photos taken at lettered positions.

A tower for light. A focal point for the house is a two-story stair tower that rises from the front foyer to the second-floor bedrooms (photo above). The floor is an inexpensive marble tile whose corners have been cut to accommodate diamond-shaped pieces in a contrasting color. Photo taken at A on floor plan.

Open risers for stair. The author's partner and his partner's brother built the open-riser staircase in just two weekends using glulam beams, oak treads and ⁵⁄₄-in. poplar salvaged from another project (photo right). Photo taken at B on floor plan.

design was the result of two principles: First, make the most of off-the-shelf technology and materials; second, create attractive details with simple tools and techniques that would not be expensive or difficult to duplicate.

One way of managing costs was to plan a simple layout for the substantial addition to the existing house. In that way, we thought, the frame would go up quickly, on-site head-scratching would be held to a minimum (any construction loan proves that time really is money), and waste in materials could be reduced. That didn't mean the finished house would lack attractive details or interesting spaces. After all, part of our purpose was to introduce potential clients to ideas they might not have seen before.

We also wanted to prove that nice touches don't have to come with big price tags—an approach to design and construction we dubbed "cheap chic." Sam and I knew that discovering how much our ideas really cost would make us better, more budget-conscious architects. There is a big difference between drawing a house on paper and actually working out the ideas on site, and we got a chance to do both.

Lot dictates house form—About two thirds of the half-acre lot is behind the house, so we had an obvious place for a large addition. But the lot's slope was a stumbling block. The house was perched about 8 ft. higher than the street in front, and the backyard rose another 8 ft. before it ended at the rear property line. Sure, we could add more square footage to the back of the house. But the farther up the slope the addition grew, the deeper it would be pushed into the ground.

The solution was to step the addition up as it moved away from the main house. We lifted the living room 1 ft. above the main floor of the existing house, then raised the adjacent dining room, kitchen and family-room addition another 1 ft. The result was a series of connected rooms that move up as they move toward the back of the property. In all, we used four 6-in. risers to link old and new parts of the house with a total difference in elevation of 2 ft. It made all the difference in the world.

We also added two second-floor bedrooms to the plan, each with its own bathroom, and placed them above the new kitchen-family room at the rear of the house. The bedrooms open onto a common second-story deck that looks out over the backyard. To reach the second floor, we decided stairs would ascend through a two-story tower beginning in the first-floor foyer (photos this page). On the tower's two outside walls, windows would rise in a building-block pattern, bringing light into the building's interior on both the first and second floors. The tower looks something like a lighthouse from the outside (photo p. 72), especially at night.

Finally, the old cinder-block garage had to go. We replaced it with a new, two-bay garage, which was lowered in elevation so that it would be closer to street height. That would help reduce the pitch of the steep driveway. The garage also gave us enough room to add a small shop.

The addition we planned was 2,600-sq. ft. (floor plan p. 73). But it still left plenty of room at the

Dormers for the inside. The architects designed drywall dormers for the wall that separates the den-nursery from a hall. The dormers light the long hallway and give the room some architectural interest. Photo taken at C on floor plan.

back of the lot where mature plantings, including a couple of original pear and cherry trees, provide a sense of privacy (top photo, p. 77). To make the most of this outside space, we designed a series of stone retaining walls around the new wings of the house. The walls frame slate and cedar terraces that provide good views from inside the house and make it easy to get outside from any of several rooms.

A nasty construction surprise—With plans on paper (and some details still in our heads), we began construction in late September by demolishing the partially attached garage and putting in the foundations for the addition. Work on the shell of the expanded house went smoothly, until it was time to peel off the rear and left walls of the existing house and tie the house into the addition. That's when we hit our first snag.

Before we bought the house, Sam and I had wondered how difficult it would be to link the existing house with an addition. With that question in mind, Sam had opened up a section of wall to see what kind of construction we would have to deal with. As it turned out, he picked an old doorway that had been filled in with wood

framing at some time. Not illogically, Sam concluded the house was of wood-frame construction. And that's what we thought right up to the day those two walls were to be torn down.

So everyone was surprised to discover that the walls were actually concrete block. That was not an insurmountable problem. But never underestimate the difficulty of bringing new wood construction that is plumb and level into line with old, rough concrete block that is neither. We also found that the original rough-sawn wood joists and rafters had absorbed so much moisture over the years that few of them were still straight.

Block by block, stud by stud, and kicking and screaming the whole way, we slowly replaced most of the original structure. Hindsight now tells us that it would have been simpler and quicker to take the house down to the first-floor deck and start again. But we had become captives of our own plan. In trying to salvage as much as possible, we didn't save either the time or the materials we thought we would.

A mix of styles inside—Part of our plan was to use the rebuilt house as a sort of design library that featured many ideas. Our office would be

in the house (it has since moved down the street), and we wanted to show potential clients a mix of architectural styles just by taking a walk around the house. With some planning, for example, we were able to work in four different ceiling styles throughout the house.

In the den-nursery—a long room facing the street (photo above)—one side of the vaulted ceiling is formed by the underside of the roof rafters. This slope is matched on the opposite side of the room by nonstructural ceiling joists slanting down from the room's centerline to the inside wall that separates the room from an adjoining hall. Two doorways open to the hall, and above each of them we formed a drywall dormer complete with a window. With a wall of windows on one side and the two dormers on the other, the room feels almost like a freestanding structure. Viewed from the hall, the dormers add visual interest and light to what would otherwise be an oppressively dark tunnel leading to the master bedroom.

What we call a "tray ceiling" in the master bedroom is really a coffered ceiling that creates a recessed area between two ceiling planes where we installed fluorescent lights. The resulting

Marble at a reasonable cost. **By sorting through boxes of less expensive marble tile, the author and his partner matched grain and textures at a fraction of the cost of marble slab. The ceiling is dominated by a site-built light fixture of oak and opaque Plexiglas. Photo taken at D on floor plan.**

valance and the white ceiling and walls spread the light and softly illuminate the room.

In the kitchen we turned a flat ceiling into a light fixture (photo above). We built an oak frame consisting of 15 connected squares 2 ft. on a side, each fitted with a piece of opaque Plexiglas below. Ordinary shop lights, 8-ft. fluorescent tubes, mounted on the ceiling provide the light. Then we added four adjustable spotlights for more directed lighting in key kitchen work areas. The result is a bright ceiling background and attractive task lights that can be swiveled to suit individual needs. Once again, the technique was not especially expensive or time-consuming.

In the foyer we stuck with a plain, flat ceiling. But it opens directly to the stair tower, and because of its height (19 ft. from the floor to the top of the tower), the ceiling gives the foyer an airy, open feeling while directing lots of light into the interior of the house.

Most of these designs were simple to do. All but one are drywall-finished shapes. We found

them economical to build, but we also discovered that drywall demands fairly close tolerances in both rough framing and finishing to keep intersecting lines straight.

Using windows to advantage—We installed standard windows wherever we could to control costs, using custom windows only where necessary. In the stair tower we used standard-sized windows like blocks of light, stepping them up the walls in a pattern that echoes the shape of the addition and its terraces (photo p. 72). In the kitchen we were forced to order custom windows because they had to match the cabinet widths exactly, and off-the-shelf windows were the wrong size. But we softened the financial blow by ordering simple, fixed units. It wasn't cheap, but it gave us the most for our buck.

Getting light far into the house while protecting the privacy of those inside was another important challenge. Part of the answer was to push windows in some rooms up as close to the top plate as possible, making windows that appear headerless. Curtains could then be drawn across lower windows or door units while the upper windows remain unblocked. To build these windows, we incorporated headers directly into the roof framing. We used the technique in three rooms: in the den-nursery, in the living room and in the kitchen over the cabinets.

Where there is no eave, this detail is quite simple. We just put the header on top of the top plate of the perimeter wall and, using joist hangers, brought the rafters into the side of the header. Where an overhang is needed, the header is moved out to become a subfascia. By carefully placing rafters at both ends of a run of windows and over solid bearing, these end rafters act as cantilevered beams to support the header-subfascia pieces. The headers hold up common rafters set into them.

This headerless window was a real puzzler for our local building inspector. We were finally able to explain it to his satisfaction only after providing two sets of supplemental details, several 3-D diagrams, structural calculations and a complete, full-size mockup, with the whole building crew providing an on-the-spot weight test (for more on the technique, see *FHB* #75, p. 84).

The look without the price—Our architectural firm handles a range of projects, from big to small. Everyone has a budget that has to be squeezed for the maximum value and best-looking result. We were no exception, and we looked everywhere for ways to get "that look" without "that price." Our favorite example is the continuous green marble backsplash in the kitchen. The marble's color and texture add tremendously to the room but only cost an additional $392.

Look closely before you scoff. That isn't custom-cut slab stock, which would have cost $1,500 or more. It's actually marble tile. The bookmatching was the key to getting this to look like a far more expensive job—and it's usually possible to do with a box of standard marble tile. Marble tile is cut from a slab of rock and then boxed. All you have to do is lay out the entire box on the floor and figure out the puzzle. It doesn't always

Room to grow in back. The backyard offered plenty of room for expansion and privacy, once the architects found a way to deal with the sloping lot. Upstairs, the bedrooms open onto a deck that is covered with concrete pavers over a membrane roof. Below the deck is the family room and the breakfast nook. To the left is the living room.

work out exactly, but you'll be surprised at how often it's possible to match grains and patterns in the tile so that a wall or a backsplash looks like a single piece of stone. We used the same strategy for matching red marble tile in the master-bedroom bath (photo below right).

Another cheap-chic design is the marble floor in the main entry. This amount of marble normally would be a real luxury for a tight budget. But we used lower-grade ⅜-in. Carrara-type marble, with lots of variation in color. We also laid it roughly, like quarry tile, without trying to join all the edges perfectly. This gave us some extra time and money to work a diamond pattern in the foyer floor that was very much in keeping with the other details of the house. We saved money by renting a masonry saw and nipping off the corners of the tile for the diamond pattern ourselves, instead of asking the installer to do it.

Because of its central location, the stair tower and staircase would be a focal point for the house, and we wanted something dramatic. Without spending a fortune, Sam and his brother Marion built the L-shaped stair (photos p. 74) in just a weekend or two. The lower flight is fairly traditional, but the upper flight is an open-riser design that lets light from the windows penetrate deep into the house. The two stringers for the upper flight are 15-in. deep glulam beams, and the treads are 2x oak members that we had edged at a local cabinet shop to enhance the feeling that the stair treads are floating.

The balusters were cut down from ⁵⁄₄-in. poplar stock from another project, and we bundled the same material together to form the newel posts. The contrasting wooden cubes that top the balusters were cut from scrap ⁵⁄₄-in. oak and stained in a warm tone as a tie-in to the contrasting marble diamonds in the foyer floor. The handrail itself is simply an oak 2x4 that we ran through the table saw four times to give it a knifelike shape on its two edges. Two final passes put in a kerf line that makes the rail easier to grip. □

Jack Wilbern is a partner in The Butz-Wilbern Partnership, an architectural firm in McLean, Va. Photos by Scott Gibson except where noted.

Light plus privacy. Windows located high on the gable wall bring plenty of light into the master bath without sacrificing privacy. The glass-block shower helps diffuse the light. Photo taken at E on floor plan.

Adding a Second Story

You can save time and avoid weather worries by building the new roof before tearing off the old one

by Tony Simmonds

It was a wonderful, prematurely warm day at the beginning of March 1994 when I first met Paul and Letizia Myers to discuss adding a second story to their house (photo right). Both of their children were in their teens, and the house was beyond feeling cramped. A second story would give Paul and Letizia a master suite, a room for each child and another bathroom.

That sunny March day had the kind of morning when tearing off the roof seems like the most natural and logical thing in the world. In fact, as Paul and I stood in the warm sun and looked at the roof he had repeatedly patched with elastomeric compounds, it seemed an unreasonable strain on anybody's patience to formulate a program, draw plans and apply for permits.

In reality, the timing should have been perfect. The design could get done, and the plans drawn, in time to begin construction by late summer. August and September are the most reliably dry time of year in Vancouver.

But events foiled us. A strike at City Hall slowed the permitting process, and it was into November by the time we had approval to go ahead. Reluctantly, we shelved the project until spring. Then I met contractor Walter Ilg.

It's just too small. Charming in its simplicity and located in a good part of town, this one-story house had been outgrown by its owners. Adding a second story solved the space problem, and using simple construction methods, including prefabricated trusses, kept the total cost to just over $100,000 (Canadian).

Walter makes a specialty of handling what he calls "the hard parts" of any renovation. I watched his crew remove and replace the foundation of my neighbor's house, and I was impressed with the expeditious way he handled the hard part of that one. So I showed him the plans for the Myerses' project. We agreed that the way to do it was to put up the new roof be-

fore taking down the old one. But we disagreed about timing. I had in mind the end of April. "Why wait?" he said. "It can rain anytime here."

It could do more than that, as were to find out. But on a warm Monday in March, almost exactly a year after my first visit with the Myerses, Walter and his crew started building scaffolding.

Prefab trusses and minimal walls help the new roof go up quickly—Walter's theory of framing is simple. You do the minimum necessary to get the roof on, throw a party and then back-frame the rest. In this case the minimum was less than it might have been because the existing attic floor framing—2x8s on 16-in. centers—didn't have to be reinforced. Not that the job couldn't have been done the same way even if the existing joists had needed upgrading.

The new roof was also designed with minimums in mind: minimum cost and minimum delay. There would be no stick-framing; instead, factory-supplied trusses would carry the loads down the outside walls. Almost half of the trusses would be scissor trusses for the exposed wood ceiling over the stairs and in the master bedroom. The 12-in-12 pitch apron that forms

Preparing for the new roof. The crew begins construction of the new roof by excavating post holes in the old roof over the wall plate. On the left, a ramp for removing roof debris leads to a curbside Dumpster.

Posts carry a wall beam. Well-braced with diagonal 2x4s, 4x4 posts rise from the holes in the roof to support a doubled 2x10 beam. Note the temporary flashings that are at the base of the posts. At the far end, the wall beam extends beyond the plane of the house to create a staging area for the roof trusses.

The old roof comes down. With the new roof in place, the old one can come down. Next, the missing studs in the perimeter walls will be installed.

the overhang at the gables and at the ground-floor eaves would be framed after the new roof was on and the exterior walls built.

To get the roof on, we needed just two bearing walls. But a continuous wall plate couldn't be installed without severing the old roof from its bearing. The solution was to use posts and beams, and to frame in the walls afterward.

Based on the layout of the interior walls, Walter and I decided to use four 4x4 posts along each side of the house. The beams would be doubled 2x10s. In one place, one beam would have to span almost 16 ft., but any deflection could easily be taken out when the permanent

wall was framed underneath it. As it turned out, there wasn't any.

So on Tuesday morning, with the scaffolding built, Walter's crew cut four pockets in the appropriate locations along each side of the roof (top photo). Then they secured the 4x4 posts to the existing floor framing and to the top plate of the wall below. They notched the end posts to fit into the corner made by the end joist and the rim joist. We were lucky with the intermediate ones; all of them could be fastened directly to a joist, notching the bottom of the 4x4 as required. None of the four intermediate locations was so critical, though, that the post couldn't have been

moved a few inches in one direction or the other if necessary.

Walter used a builder's level to establish the height of the posts, and by Tuesday afternoon one of the beams was up and braced back to the existing roof (photo bottom left), and the posts were in place for the other one.

At the same time, the rest of the crew was cutting away the ridge of the existing roof to allow the flat bottom chord of the common trusses to pass across (top photo, facing page). They were able to leave the old attic collar ties/ceiling joists in place, though, because the old ceiling had been only 7 ft. 6 in. I stopped by at the end of the

A roof apron recalls the original proportions. Strong diagonal lines drawn by the 12-in-12 rake boards at the gable ends help to break up what would otherwise be a top-heavy facade. The lower roof continues across the front and back of the house, sheltering the windows and preserving the original roofline.

Bump-out and fascias support the rake soffit. At the gable end, a bump-out protects the upstairs windows and supports the tops of the 2x10 bargeboards. The 2x10s are borne by 2x6 fascias cantilevered past the roof-apron rafters. Note how a built-up water table makes a clean line between the old stucco and the new.

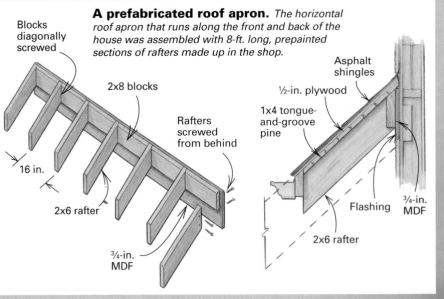

A prefabricated roof apron. *The horizontal roof apron that runs along the front and back of the house was assembled with 8-ft. long, prepainted sections of rafters made up in the shop.*

Blocks diagonally screwed

2x8 blocks

Rafters screwed from behind

16 in.

2x6 rafter

¾-in. MDF

Asphalt shingles

½-in. plywood

1x4 tongue-and-groove pine

Flashing

¾-in. MDF

2x6 rafter

Drawings: Bob La Pointe

day to inspect the temporary post flashings the crew had made with poly and duct tape. It had been another sunny day. By afternoon, however, thin clouds had moved in, and it was getting cold. The forecast was for snow.

Snow and rain complicated the job—The order for the trusses had been placed the previous week, with delivery scheduled for Thursday or Friday. But on Monday, while we were overseeing the lumber delivery, Walter let me know that he had called the truss company and promised them a case of beer if they delivered the trusses on Thursday and three cases if they got them here by Wednesday.

On Wednesday morning there was 8 in. of snow on the ground—and on the Myerses' roof. But the weather system had blown right through, and by 8 a. m. the snow was melting fast. Walter called to say he had sent two men to sweep the snow off the roof and that the trusses would be on site if the truck could make it out of the yard. At noon I arrived to see the last bundle of trusses being landed on temporary outrigger beams.

The rest of that day was spent finishing the beam, and setting and bracing the trusses. Plywood laid across where the old ridge had been scalped made it easy for one man to walk down the roof supporting the center of the truss while two others walked it along the scaffolding.

Even though it violated Walter's get-it-done roofing rule, I had the crew install the frieze blocking as the trusses were installed. By cutting the blocks with a chopsaw, you can ensure perfect spacing (even layout becomes unnecessary where framing proceeds on regular centers), and it's much easier to fasten the blocking this way than it is to go back and toe-nail it all afterward. Also, the soffit-venting detail I used with the exposed rafter tails required the screen to be sandwiched between two courses of soffit and stapled to the inside of the frieze block.

On Thursday another front brought wind and rain, which dispatched the last vestiges of snow but made a miserable day for the sheathing crew. Having to install the soffit, the screening and the 2x4 purlins that tie all of the trusses together didn't speed things up. Nor did the four skylights. I didn't want the bargeboards done hurriedly, so to make things easier for the roofers, we temporarily toe-nailed 2x4s on the flat to the trimmed ends of the rake soffits. That way, the roofers could cut their shingles flush to the outside edge of the 2x4, and when the 2x4s were removed and replaced by the permanent 2x10 bargeboard and 1x3 crown, the shingles would overhang by a consistent 1¼-in. margin.

On Friday morning the roofers went to work on one side of the roof while the last nails were pounded into the sheathing on the other side. It didn't take long for them to lay the 12 squares we needed to make everything waterproof. Meanwhile, Walter and his crew were removing the old roof underneath (photo bottom right, p. 79) and carrying it to the Dumpster in 4-ft. by 12-ft. chunks. I usually try to save the old rafters, but in this case I'm afraid I let the momentum of the job dictate the recycling policy.

By 1 p. m., true to his word and to long European tradition, Walter was tying an evergreen branch to the ridge, and plates of cheese, bread and sausage were being laid out on a sheet of plywood set up on sawhorses in the 26-ft. by 34-ft. pavilion that now occupied the top floor of the house. It might be a little breezy, as Paul said to me over a glass of wine, but at least it was dry.

A roof apron prevents a boxy look—It took another three weeks to complete the framing and to do all of the picky work that's an inevitable part of tying everything together in a renovation. One detail, and an important element of the design, is the roof apron that encircles the house to break up the height of the building (top photo, facing page). The apron forms an eave along the front and back of the house. At the gable ends, the apron becomes a rake that rises to the peak of the roof, drawing long diagonal lines across what would otherwise be a tall, blank facade. The effect is of a 12-in-12 roof with 4½-in-12 shed dormers.

The apron has practical value, too, particularly at the eave, where it covers the top edge of the existing wall finish, providing an overhang to protect the ground-floor windows. If you're building outside the painting season, it's essential to get a coat of paint on everything before it's applied to the outside of the house, so we built as much as we could of this apron in 8-ft. sections in my shop (drawing facing page). For example, the eaves consist of 2-ft. long 2x6 lookout rafters screwed from the back to a 12-in. wide strip of Medex (Medite Corp., P. O. Box

Daylight in the center of the house. Skylights over the centrally located hallway light up the stairs, as well as the bathroom, by way of its generous transom. Photo taken at A on floor plan.

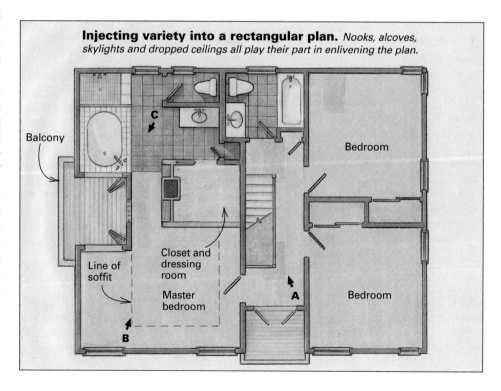

Injecting variety into a rectangular plan. *Nooks, alcoves, skylights and dropped ceilings all play their part in enlivening the plan.*

Balcony

C

Bedroom

Line of soffit

Closet and dressing room

Master bedroom

A

Bedroom

B

4040, Medford, Ore. 97501; 541-773-2522), an exterior-grade medium-density fiberboard that is gaining popularity for use as exterior trim here. Frieze blocks cut from 2x8s act as pressure blocks between the rafters. We prepainted these assemblies and the 1x4 tongue-and-groove pine that we nailed to their tops in our shop.

On site, the eave sections were installed and tied together with the prepainted 1x4s and 2x6 fascia. Then we snapped lines on the gable ends from the ridge to the eave lookouts to establish the line of the rake soffit (bottom photo, p. 80). On this line, we toe-nailed a triangular bump-out, framed out of 2x10s, to the gable-wall framing. From the base of the bump-out, we ran a 2x6 that acts as a rake trim board for most of its length and then becomes the last lookout rafter where it runs into the eave overhang.

We nailed preassembled and prepainted strips of soffit to the rake trim and to the gable bump-out. Made of tongue-and-groove 1x4s blind-nailed to 18-in. wide strips of ½-in. plywood, the 8-ft. long strips of rake soffit were pretty floppy until the 2x10 bargeboards went on.

Projecting the gable peaks out from the plane of the wall did more than provide solid support for the rake apron with its heavy bargeboard. It also created some visual interest and gave a little protection to the bedroom windows in the east wall. The peaks were finished with louvered vents and 1x4 bevel siding. These peaks make a nice big triangle of painted woodwork to balance the large areas of stucco.

We also ran a water table at the second-floor joist level (bottom photo, p. 80). Besides its aesthetic contribution, this band covers the flashing protecting the top edge of the old stucco and makes a practical separation so that new stucco and old don't have to meet. Detailing woodwork so that stucco always has a place to stop and so that no one panel of it is too big makes the plasterer's job a whole lot easier.

Shaun Friedrich, who learned the stucco trade from his father and who can tell without leaving his truck what a particular stucco is, when it was done and quite often who did it, made a beautiful job of approximating the look of the original dry-dash finish. Dry dash is a labor-intensive stucco finish in which a layer of small, sharp stones is embedded in a layer of mortar. Shaun rendered a compatible finish for the upstairs walls by using a drywall-texturing gun to create the random, splattered look of dry dash. This substitution saved us $1,000.

Allocating the new space—On the inside, Walter's crew was turning the 26-ft. by 34-ft. pavilion into a second floor with three bedrooms and two baths (floor plan, p. 81). The west end contains a master bedroom and bath. In the center

The outdoors is nearby. On the left, folding windows lead to a balcony off the master suite. On the right, a 7-ft. closet wall separates bedroom from lavatory. The sloping ceiling extends beyond the ridge to become part of the skylight well over the closet. Photo taken at B on floor plan.

of the house, a hallway includes the existing stair, a bathroom at the north end (photo p. 81) and a balcony at the south end. Bedrooms at the east end complete the plan.

The subdivision of the master-bedroom space to accommodate a walk-in closet and the bathroom was the most intriguing part of the design. I wanted the room to feel large and generously proportioned, but at the same time I wanted the different areas within it to be well-defined.

The first division is between north and south. The bathroom, with its requirement for privacy, is on the north side; the bedroom is on the south. What separates them is not a wall but other subsidiary spaces: the walk-in closet and a small balcony (photo facing page).

Then there is the division between the main part of the room and the three 6-ft. deep alcoves along the west wall. Linked by their common ceiling height—7 ft.—the alcoves contain from north to south the shower/tub space; the balcony; and the bedroom-dresser area.

In addition to their common ceiling heights, the alcoves are further linked by large windows that open onto the balcony (photo above). These windows can be folded back against the

A balcony separates the bedroom and the bath. Along the west wall, three alcoves with low ceilings have distinct functions. In the foreground, the shower and tub occupy the first alcove. In the middle, a small balcony overlooks the secluded backyard. In the distance, the third alcove provides space for the bedroom dresser. Photo taken at C on floor plan.

wall so that in nice weather the balcony is really a part of the bedroom.

The transparency of these linked alcoves to one another goes a step farther. On the bathroom side, the shower is separated from the tub by a glass partition; on the bedroom side a window in the south wall lines up with the two windows to the balcony. Standing in the shower, you can look right through four transparent layers to the outside. In a small house, long views such as these foster a sense of spaciousness.

The ceiling in the master bedroom is an example of how to turn a technical problem to

practical advantage. The decision to use trusses throughout for the sake of expeditiousness and economy meant that the ceiling could slope only at a pitch of 2-in-12 (the bottom chord of a 4½-in-12 scissor truss), and that skylight wells would necessarily be rather deep. Locating the skylight so that the slope of one side of the ceiling extends into the skylight well to meet the top of the skylight makes for a dramatic light shaft that spills light all along the ceiling as well as down the wall (photo right, facing page). It also didn't leave much room for error in the layout we had to do back on that raw day in March

when Walter's crew members were swarming over the roof with snow in their hair and shinglers at their heels.

As for the low slope of the ceiling, we made it seem higher by holding the closet walls to a height of 7 ft. In the end the effect was everything we had hoped it would be. Letizia, who is Swiss and for whom I was trying to echo a wooden chalet ceiling, was not disappointed. □

Tony Simmonds operates Domus, a design/build firm in Vancouver, British Columbia, Canada. Photos by Charles Miller except where noted.

After. The remodel replaced the attic with a cruciform master-bedroom suite capped by a cupola that serves as a private retreat. Outside, the old, painted shingle siding was replaced by new cedar clapboards garnished with decorative shingles and sunbursts.

Going up

This speedy remodel added a master-bedroom suite

By Michael J. Crosbie

When Doug Haney and Susan Mitchell bought their house in 1984, it was two stories high, with a squat hipped roof and gray shingle siding—a rather conventional, turn-of-the-century place (photo facing page). It had, however, undergone a series of significant renovations that considerably improved the interior. Coupled with a secluded site having a seasonal view of the Connecticut River, the open, bright first-floor was a major selling point.

Unfortunately, the rest of the house was cramped. On the first floor, a stuffy little kitchen was a sorry counterpoint to the large, light-filled living areas. Upstairs were three small bedrooms and a single bath. Compounding the problem, Haney ran his computer business at home, and Mitchell brought her banking job home two days a week; they shared the smallest bedroom as their home office. Adding on to the house presented problems. Although the wooded site was secluded, property lines were tight. The boundary to the east was just 12 ft. from the house, and the septic system made the west end of the site unbuildable. The land sloped away to the north,

and to the south the house butted the driveway. The pristine nature of the house's square plan also discouraged bump-outs. Going up seemed the only alternative.

A three-story solution—Initially the couple hoped the attic space could be converted into a master-bedroom suite simply by popping a few dormers into the roof, a concept that was studied by the architectural firm I work for. Bob Harper was partner-in-charge of the project, Susan Edler-Wyeth was project architect, and the design team included Tracy Davis, William Eagan and me. We quickly determined that the 8-in-12 pitch of the roof wouldn't supply the headroom needed for a simple conversion.

The solution was to tear off the roof and to build a third story (photo left). The addition would include four dormers to accentuate the existing square plan. An 11-in-12 roof pitch and a higher eave would allow on the third floor much of the spaciousness and sunlight that Haney and Mitchell enjoyed on the first floor.

The cruciform plan of the addition (drawing below) would be perfect for accommodating a sleeping area, a sitting area, a dressing area and a master bath complete with a whirlpool tub. Each space would occupy its own quadrant, with the four quadrants arranged around a central stair and a chimney.

We added to the design something the clients hadn't requested but that appealed to them instantly—a cupola above the third floor, accessible by a ladder. The cupola would offer a very private retreat and, with windows on three of its four sides (the fourth containing the chimney), panoramic views of the town and the river.

The transformation would be completed by pulling off the existing painted shingle siding and installing clapboards over the entire house and most of the addition. The clients initially wanted to re-side the house with unpainted shingles, but the likelihood of uneven weathering dissuaded them. The sharp lines and crisp edges of clapboard siding presented a viable alternative.

Beating the weather—Haney and Mitchell planned to occupy the house during construction, conducting business as usual. Tearing off the roof to build the addition would place them and the existing interior of the house at the mercy of the weather. Fortunately, Triangle Building Associates, Inc., the local builders who tackled the addition, devised a clever plan that minimized the risk.

Conceived by Harper and Russell Smith, Triangle's hands-on president, the plan was to remove the existing roof and frame enough of the addition to support reinforced polyethylene tarps—all in one day. The strategy was pretty straightforward: Prefabricate the walls for the addition on site and then use a crane to lift off the existing roof and raise the prefabricated components into place. The crane would remove the old roof in large chunks. Prefabrication (all of it done on site) would take about a week, and the crane would complete the lifting in one day at a cost of $750.

The repetitive nature of the addition's elements—four equal dormers with a square cupola on top—made prefabrication a snap. All exterior walls were framed with 2x4s spaced 16 in. o. c. and sheathed with ⅝-in. plywood. A square opening framed into each of the dormer sidewalls would give the carpenters easy access to the outside corners of the addition for framing small hip roofs between the dormers. The 2x8 rafters for the dormers were also precut, and eight ladders were assembled to serve as the gable-end roof overhangs. A simple 2x4 cage was framed for supporting the cupola, and finally, the cupola

Before. **When the Haney-Mitchell's bought their conventional turn-of-the-century house, it had plenty of room in its living areas but lacked a real master bedroom. Photo by Doug Haney.**

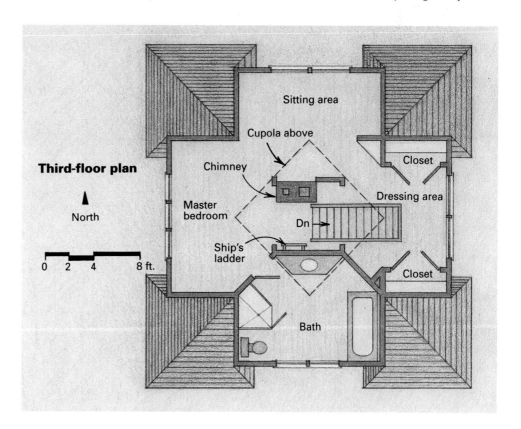

Third-floor plan

▲ North

0 2 4 8 ft.

Sitting area

Cupola above

Chimney

Closet

Master bedroom

Dressing area

Dn →

Ship's ladder

Closet

Bath

floor was framed with 2x8 joists spaced 16 in. o. c. and decked with ¾-in. plywood.

Meanwhile, Triangle's crew removed the existing shingle siding on the house and then covered the exposed sheathing with Tyvek housewrap. The crew also dismantled the existing single-flue, brick chimney down to the smoke chamber of the first-floor fireplace. This chimney would later be replaced by a double-flue chimney (where one flue serves a furnace and the other a fireplace) that would extend through the cupola roof.

With the chimney out of the way, a new floor was built in the attic. Originally, the idea was to sister new floor joists to existing joists to beef up the structure, but Smith was worried that the plaster in the second-floor ceilings might crack in the process. Instead, a new floor of 2x8 joists decked with ¾-in. plywood was built on top of the attic floor. Because the roof was supported at its perimeter by beams raised about 6 in. above the existing attic floor, the new floor could butt into the beams without bumping into the existing rafters. Once the roof was torn off, a 2x4 plate

Craning day. To limit exposure of the existing interior, a crane lifted the old roof off and then hoisted the prefabricated walls of the addition onto the new third-floor deck (photo above). The addition was sealed tightly enough to resist a heavy downpour that night. Photo by Doug Haney.

Shaping the cornice. The coved cornice of the cupola was achieved by cutting curves in a series of 2x10 blocks, nailing the blocks to the eaves and then nailing 1x3 strips of T&G Western red cedar horizontally to the blocks.

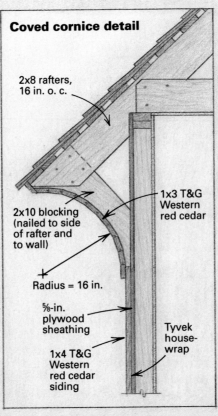

Coved cornice detail

2x8 rafters, 16 in. o. c.

1x3 T&G Western red cedar

2x10 blocking (nailed to side of rafter and to wall)

Radius = 16 in.

⅝-in. plywood sheathing

1x4 T&G Western red cedar siding

Tyvek house-wrap

would be nailed to the tops of the beams to bring them flush with the new subfloor. To compensate for raising the floor, Triangle added one riser to the existing third-floor stair.

Off with its roof—To everyone's relief, the morning of lift-off dawned with a clear sky. Now it was time to put the grand plan to the test.

Smith describes his strategy for removing the roof as "the soft-boiled-egg routine—take off the top and then peel away the rest." Smith's crew used reciprocating saws to make a number of cuts in the roof. This produced nine separate roof sections: the peak, four hip sections and four midsections (which included two small dormers). Where necessary, temporary 2x4 bracing was installed in the attic to shore up the roof. With the cuts completed, holes were cut in each section to allow a cable to be threaded through.

Smith hired Bombaci Tree Experts and Crane Service of Essex, Connecticut, to do the lifting. Their heavy lifter is a 12-ton capacity, 105-ft. long telescoping crane planted in the chassis of a Ford F-800 truck. The crane lifted the peak off first, then worked its way counterclockwise around the roof to remove the hips and the midsections. When lifting the eight bottom sections, the crane operator gently rocked each one to loosen the nails at the plate line. This method, as opposed to ripping the sections straight up, minimized stress on the walls below and helped prevent the interior plaster from cracking. Upon removal, each roof section was placed neatly next to a dumpster, cut into smaller pieces and deposited. The entire process took about an hour.

With the roof off, Smith's crew quickly nailed 2x4 plates to the tops of the perimeter beams and laid out the deck to ensure proper alignment of the prefabricated parts. When hoisting the prefabricated components, the crane worked its way from the back of the house toward the front to avoid collisions. The east gable wall was raised, positioned and nailed down, then braced to the deck until its two sidewalls were installed. Next, the supporting cage for the cupola was installed directly over the stairwell on the third floor. That done, the north dormer was installed, followed by the south and west dormers.

With the dormers up, the prefabricated cupola floor was lifted and placed on top of the cage and rotated 45° so that its doubled rim joists were supported at midspan by the corners of the cage. The four cupola walls were then hoisted and installed (photo left). The cupola's load is transferred down through the cube to the balloon-framed walls of the existing stairwell. These walls extend to the first floor where they're supported by double 2x10 beams that rest on Lally columns bolted to the basement slab.

With the cupola walls up, Smith's crew nailed up temporary 2x ridge beams to support a reinforced polyethylene tarp. It was secured with nylon rope just as storm clouds appeared on the horizon. Sure enough, it rained hard and steady that night, but only a tiny amount of water trickled into the house.

Diamonds and sunbursts—The rest of the framing was completed quickly. For visual interest, the clapboard siding was installed 2½ in. to the weather below the first-floor window sills and 4½ in. to the weather up to the tympanums (triangular tops) of the four gable walls. The tympanums are filled with clapboard sunbursts (for more on making sunbursts, see *FHB #51, p. 14*). Three of the gable ends are fitted with two 6-ft. high, double-hung windows. The west gable end, however, has three 2-ft. high awning windows placed high in the wall for privacy in the bedroom. To balance the gables visually, a 4-ft. by 6-ft. square of decorative shingles was nailed up directly beneath the awning windows.

The cupola is finished with 1x4 T&G Western red cedar siding, installed vertically. Three of the cupola walls have identical awning windows, while the northwest wall (adjacent to the chimney) harbors a 3-ft. square field of decorative shingles. The cupola's singular feature, however, is its coved cornice (photo and drawing facing page). The cornice was built by cutting 16-in. radius curves into a series of 2x10 blocks, nailing the blocks to the eaves and then nailing 1x3 strips of T&G Western red cedar to the blocks. Compound miters were cut at the corners and trimmed with a ¼-in. by ¾-in. strip of plain molding.

The understated color scheme for the exterior is patterned after that of a nearby house. (The

Twisting in the bedroom. The core of the addition is occupied by the main stairwell and a two-flue chimney that twists and corbels from the first-floor fireplace to the cupola before exiting through the cupola roof. At the top of the stair, a shop-built ship's ladder ascends to the cupola. When not in use, the ladder is pressed against the wall.

painter suggested a different color for every piece in the gable fans—an option the clients politely refused.)

Interior with a twist—The most dramatic feature of the third-floor interior is the new chimney, which rises straight up to the third floor from the first-floor fireplace, then twists 45° to the cupola roof while simultaneously corbeling 20 in. to the northwest (photo above).

This massive leaning tower would demand more of brick and mortar than gravity alone would allow. According to structural engineer Jim Norden, a backbone of steel was a must. This backbone would consist of four lengths of #5 rebar routed through an 8-in. by 12-in. concrete-filled channel. Originating on the east side of the fireplace, the channel would follow the convex side of the chimney through the roof, placing the steel in tension to counteract the leaning mass of the chimney. Norden also called for the addition of an 8-in. concrete-block wall on the east side of the fireplace to help counterbalance the load.

Mason Stan Bates worked out the construction details. He tied the chimney base to the fireplace by scooping out the rubble on the east side of the smokebox, inserting the bottom ends of the rebar (which were bent to right angles) into the resulting pocket, then filling the pocket with con-

crete. Bates worked with 8-ft. long rebar throughout, overlapping the joints a minimum of 24 in. and lashing them with tie wire. From the third floor up, the outside of the fireplace is a frogged composition shale brick (a frog is an indentation in the surface of a brick that interlocks with mortar) laid with high-bond strength, type S mortar.

Bates added 22.5° of the twist in the third floor and the second 22.5° in the cupola. Laying up the twisted chimney turned out to be almost as simple as laying up a straight one. Bates just ran four strings (one at each corner) from the rectangular opening in the third floor to the rectangular opening in the cupola floor. Aligning the ends of each course with the strings guaranteed the proper degree of twist in the chimney.

Bates used strings in the cupola, too. When the chimney reached the cupola ceiling, it was snug against the northeast wall. At the top Bates bent the rebar and embedded it in the chimney cap.

A chimney like this one deserves a special accent. Bates installed two decorative clay chimney pots on top (Superior Clay Corp., P. O. Box 352, Uhrichsville, Ohio 44683; 614-922-4122) that echo the shape of the gables below. ☐

Michael J. Crosbie is an architect with Centerbrook Architects in Essex, Conn. Photos by Bruce Greenlaw except where noted.

A Dramatic Family-Room Addition

A steel top plate eliminates collar ties from a cathedral ceiling, and arched dormers provide natural light

by B. Alan Leonard

New Jersey, the Garden State. Every once in a while, you come across an area of New Jersey that actually lives up to the state's nickname. Jeff and Chris Wells recently moved to such an area. Set graciously on a gently rolling, 3-acre wooded parcel near a large parkland, their home is a 35-year-old, 1½-story French-style ranch that included details both graceful and shabby. The house united the fine detailing of arched copper dormers and chimney pots with rotting board-and-batten siding; elegant chimney pots were combined with corrugated roofing on a detached garage.

The Wellses had many wishes for their new home, and they asked me to design a renovation that included adding bathrooms and changing the siding. Their greatest desire, however, was for a new room that would take full advantage of their beautiful land as well as lead to a new patio where they could entertain outdoors. The new room need not be large, but Jeff and Chris wanted it to combine a sense of excitement and elegance that defined their lifestyle.

The existing den was the best choice for a renovation because it felt dark and was not open enough to the backyard. Our first thought was to remove the rear wall and enlarge this room. But the den's 8-ft. ceiling was a problem. Had we continued the ceiling at that height, no drama. If we raised the addition's ceiling, the resulting room would be too disjointed. Our solution was to build a separate family room (19 ft. by 19 ft.) adjoining the existing den (photo top right).

Careful alignment of windows and doors—
The entrance to the den from the hallway is at one corner of the room, so the entrance to the new room aligns with the den entrance, making one side of the den into a natural circulation corridor. The family room itself is centered on its entrance, with the opposite wall containing a large window grouping that focuses on a swimming pool. Enclosed by a split-rail fence and elaborate plantings, the pool area exudes rural charm.

This visual axis is crossed by a second axis created by a stone fireplace on the north wall and a grouping of four French doors on the south wall. Decorative oval windows were placed on both sides of the doors, which open onto a new flagstone patio (photo facing page).

The fireplace creates a strong termination to the view from the patio. Because stone is massive and heavy, the fireplace also helps to weigh down the height of the room.

Hipped cathedral with dormers intensifies structural issues—The ceiling is high, nearly 20 ft. With arched dormers and no collar ties in the ceiling, the room is dramatic. Designing and building this roof offered challenges that appealed to me and to the framers, Kevin and Paul Delaney of Long Valley, New Jersey.

One of the strongest visual features of the main house is its mansard roof. Beginning at the second floor, the roof rises approximately 12 ft. at a 21-in-12 pitch, terminating in a flat roof. To maintain the character of the house, I designed an identical mansard roof for the addition. The new

No structural members pierce the cathedral ceiling. Thanks to a band of steel angle iron around the walls, the 18-ft. high cathedral ceiling in this room addition remains unobstructed by collar ties. Arched dormers and white paint also contribute to the room's light and airy feeling.

A mansard roof is a hip with a flat top. Framed with 2x10 rafters that rise at a pitch of 21-in-12, this roof is capped by a square framework of doubled 2x10s. The steel angle that resists the rafters' outward thrust is visible along the top of the walls.

Dormers create concentrated loads. The main structural supports for this roof are the doubled rafters, or primary frames, that flank the dormers. At the peak, these rafters sandwich a 4x8 roof joist, which is why they are spaced apart by blocking. Simpson HL76 steel angles tie the primary frames to the wall plates.

Hip rafters tuck under the subfascia. A platform of crisscrossing 2x8s, ringed by a double 2x10 subfascia, caps off the mansard roof. At the top, the doubled-up hip rafter is sandwiched and carried by a pair of 2x8 outriggers running on a diagonal.

Welded corners keep the walls plumb. The top plate contains continuous 3-in. by 5-in. by ½-in. steel angle between layers of 2x6s. The entire plate is through bolted, and the corners are butted together and welded.

roof extends approximately 20 ft. above grade and is capped off with what is essentially a flat roof (bottom photo, p. 89). Had we carried the hip to its natural peak, it would have towered over the existing house, soaring out of proportion and violating the scale of the new room.

Inside, the roof shell is exposed, resulting in a hipped cathedral ceiling. I have designed many gable-style cathedrals, and they are relatively simple: Use a structural ridge beam supported at either end, or use some sort of exposed collar ties near plate height to keep the weight of the room from spreading the outside walls. A hipped cathedral, however, needs to resist splaying in two directions, so a structural ridge cannot be used. Exposed collar ties would work; however, they would need to run in two directions. Much too bulky for a room of this size, a gridwork of exposed ties would tend to feel like a ceiling. The roof had to be built without collar ties.

Bringing in natural light was also an issue. Most cathedral ceilings tend to feel dark and heavy unless light is introduced. In this roof, dormers not only illuminate the ceiling space, but they also add architectural planes that catch light differently throughout the day, creating a dynamic spatial quality in the room.

Outside, the dormers have a positive impact by breaking up the roof area. Their arched roofs and windows continue the design language of the existing house dormers. But the rough openings for the dormers would also concentrate the roof loads at certain points along the top plate and further complicate the framing.

A steel tension ring keeps the walls from spreading—The purpose of collar ties is to resist the outward thrust of the rafters and to prevent the exterior walls from splaying out. Eliminating collar ties meant we had to come up with another way of keeping the walls plumb. A steel tension ring was the answer. Sandwiched into the walls' top plates, a band of steel angle iron reinforces the walls, and it prevents them from splaying.

The Delaneys framed the 9-ft. high walls with 2x6 studs, which are sturdier than 2x4s and allowed for additional insulation. The 2x6s for the double top plate were ripped down ½ in. to provide clearance for the continuous 3-in. by 5-in. by ½-in. steel angles. The Delaneys' crew lifted the angles into place and welded them together at the corners (photo bottom left). A third 2x6 was added to provide nailing for the rafters; then the entire plate was through bolted. I will always remember seeing Raphael, one of the carpenters, sitting on his drill atop the wall, boring holes through the steel-reinforced top plate.

Core of roof frame is a pair of oversize rafters and joists—Working from scaffolding set up in the new room, the crew framed the roof starting with a pair of oversize rafters and joists, or primary frames, that flank the dormers on the north and south slopes (drawing facing page). Each primary frame consists of two 2x10 rafters bolted to a 4x8 LVL (laminated veneer lumber) beam serving as a roof joist. The primary frames, spaced with blocking along their length, are bolted to the plate with heavy angles (top photo, facing page). Then the primary frames were tied together with a subfascia of doubled 2x10s. Other than between the primary frames, all roof framing is supported by these two frames.

Due to the location of the dormers flanking the chimney on the north wall, we could not align the primary frames with the sides of the flat roof. Instead, the frames are set back into the flat section, and a system of 2x8 outriggers extends out from the 4x8s to the subfascia. The outriggers pick up the 2x10 rafters on the east and west slopes, which are connected to the outriggers with clinched 20d nails. Clinching means using oversize nails that punch through the wood and are bent to keep all layers tight. There are double 2x8 outriggers at the corners that pick up the hip rafters (center photo, facing page). All rafters are joined to the wall plate with framing anchors, as are the outriggers to the 4x8s and the subfascia.

The flat roof is framed with 2x8s running parallel to the primary frames with solid blocking between to stiffen the frame. Strips of 2x material ripped on an angle provide for drainage. (The flat roof's pitch is actually about 1-in-12.) These strips also create a space above the roof insulation for air to flow from soffit vents to a cupola. Not only does the copper-roofed cupola handle the venting, but it is also a visual tie-in to the existing cupola on the garage roof.

By stiffening the connections between the roof frame and the wall as well as between the flat roof and the sloped rafters, we have a strong system that resists the outward thrusts of the roof. The steep pitch also helped; snow loading is limited to the flat section. The sloped sections are subject more to wind loads than to snow loads.

Bands of trim mediate ceiling height—
Although the roof dormers bring light into the upper reaches of the ceiling, more needed to be done to temper the height of the room. An 18-ft. ceiling in a 19-ft. by 19-ft. room feels high! Two oversize bands of moldings—one 12-in. wide crown detail at plate height and another 7½-in. wide crown at approximately 15 ft. above the floor—break the ceiling into smaller sections.

Constructed of stock components, both crowns are blocked out from the walls and roof to allow for concealed lighting. I specified continuous incandescent strip lighting on separate dimmer circuits. The top band lights the flat ceiling, and the lower band lights the sloped ceilings.

Installing a 6-in. colonial base and a 4-in. chair rail at 36 in. above the floor gives added visual weight. The stone-veneer fireplace with its large wood mantel anchors the room as does the dark green paint on the walls with a lighter ceiling. As a finishing touch, there's a walnut strip border in the oak flooring.

The new room is comfortable for entertaining. People tend to gravitate to it both for the views outside and for the views inside. The most satisfying comments suggest that the room doesn't just fit the house, it completes it. Such is the goal and the reward. ☐

B. Alan Leonard is an architect in New Providence, N. J. Photos by the author except where noted.

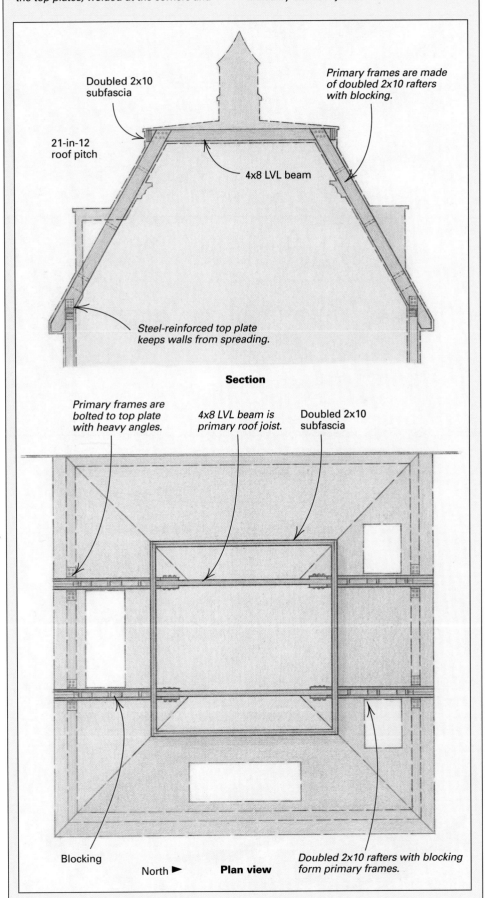

A hip roof with a flat top

Two factors complicated the framing of this roof. First, neither a structural ridge nor collar ties could be used to resist the outward thrust of the rafters. Instead, the walls are reinforced with 3-in. by 5-in. steel angle, sandwiched in the top plates, welded at the corners and acting as a tension ring. Second, four dormers pierce the roof and concentrate point loads at certain points along the top plate. The solution here was to support the roof with two pairs of primary frames, or rafters, linked by 4x8 roof joists.

Doubled 2x10 subfascia

Primary frames are made of doubled 2x10 rafters with blocking.

21-in-12 roof pitch

4x8 LVL beam

Steel-reinforced top plate keeps walls from spreading.

Section

Primary frames are bolted to top plate with heavy angles.

4x8 LVL beam is primary roof joist.

Doubled 2x10 subfascia

Blocking

North ▶   **Plan view**

Doubled 2x10 rafters with blocking form primary frames.

A Weekend Retreat

A two-story addition, plenty of windows and a dash of whimsy transform a drab cottage into a lakeside treat

by David Borenstein

Second floor

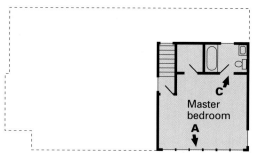

First floor

Original plan

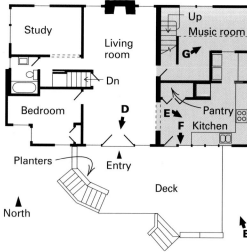

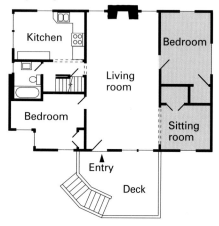

North

0 2 4   8 ft.

Photos taken at lettered positions.

Room to unwind
The poorly built bedroom and sitting room on the rear of the existing house (shaded area, bottom left) were torn off to make room for a two-story addition (shaded area, top and center left). Now the house has a new master-bedroom suite, a bright new kitchen, a music room and an expanded deck off the living room and kitchen.

The task was both straightforward and complicated. My client owned a dark and damp little lake house, and she wanted me to expand it into a light and airy weekend retreat. That was the straightforward part. The complicated part of the job was how to do it.

In the early spring of 1991, the client approached me to build the addition to her weekend house in upstate New York. On a sunny day in March, I drove over and had a look. The existing house had a few nice details, but it needed a lot of work. Also, the steeply sloped site would make construction challenging.

A boxy house on a hill, but a great view— Because the house was to serve as a vacation home and weekend retreat from New York City, the final design would have to help undo city-induced strain and stress. The client wanted the boxy and plain existing house to take on a warm, informal, relaxed feeling, a feeling she could enjoy whether she was inside or outside the house.

To create a successful design, we put a lot of thought into the choice of materials. We also concentrated on certain crucial design issues,

Drawings: Dan Thornton

An upstairs bedroom with a view. Putting the two-story addition on the rear of the house took planning and work (photo above taken at B on floor plan), but it saved a number of trees and kept the view intact from the first floor and the second-story master bedroom. The master-bedroom suite (inset photo, facing page, taken at A on floor plan), with walls full of windows, has the feeling of a room built in the trees.

such as maintaining privacy and good views of the lake, careful detailing of the way the addition worked with the landscape and smoothly combining the new with the old.

Although we needed to tie the addition carefully into the existing building, we also needed to give the new part the feel of being a separate building, not something simply added on. With that in mind, we decided it was important to treat each room in the house as a separate place, not merely as a subdivision of a larger house. The price of the remodel was to be $68,044, excluding kitchen cabinets and soffit work.

Building onto the rear saves trees and keeps the front view unobstructed—The addition was to include a new kitchen with pantry and laundry room, and a large master-bedroom suite with a walk-in closet and bathroom. With all of these considerations in mind, I went to the drawing board. For economy, I planned the addition as rectangular spaces on a 2-ft. module.

To give the client everything she wanted in the addition, I needed to increase the size of the house by 830 sq. ft. (floor plan, facing page).

Because there was only enough room for a small footprint, we decided to make one part of the addition two stories and to make the upper level smaller than the lower.

We placed the addition at the rear of the existing building. This plan saved most of the trees, maintained an unobstructed view of the lake from the small front yard and promised to preserve some privacy in the tightly built lake community (photo above). It also required removing a small, poorly built structure that had been added a few years after the original Depression-era house was built. To create the 18-ft. by 26-ft. footprint for the addition, we cut 10 ft. into the hillside and laid a stepped, concrete-block retaining wall/foundation.

The plan accomplished four things: The master-bedroom suite would be on the second level, which would give it the sense of being a separate, special place, sort of like a tree house for adults (photo facing page). The addition would have plenty of light and views on all four sides. The design allowed for a shed roof with skylights over the music room, which added light without sacrificing privacy on that side of the house (pho-

to bottom right, p. 95). And the scale of the addition would be in proportion to the existing building, but also would reinforce the idea that each room was its own separate, special place.

Cedar shingles and green paint help tie new to old—Construction of the addition was uneventful. However, tying the addition to the existing house proved to be more than just an issue of scale and proportion.

We could have refurbished the old building and let it keep its own general look, giving the addition a different character, as if two separate buildings had been joined. Or we could mix the old and the new into one cohesive design. We decided on the mixture of elements.

For example, the existing house was sided in cedar shingles, which are relatively mainte-

Opened to the out-of-doors. French doors create a wall of light and color in the living room and bring in a full view of the lake. Photo taken at D on floor plan.

Tucked away. The bathroom was placed on the north side of the house so that the master bedroom could be fully opened to the view on the south side. Photo taken at C on floor plan.

A wall of light. A trio of small windows behind the counter gives way to a longer window for lake views from the bench seat. Photo taken at E on floor plan.

nance-free, so we sided the addition with the same material. The cedar shingles also made it possible to build in the flared skirt, which makes a subtle visual transition between the building and the foundation.

The exterior-trim details of the new, particularly the fascia and soffits, were added to the old, which allowed us to replace rotted wood and to correct general deterioration of the eaves. Fascias and soffits were stained green and were wrapped around the building, reinforcing the lines of the roofs and unifying the whole.

Windows vary views and give rooms a unique feel—One way to give each room the feeling of being a separate place was to use an

Free-form trim work. The organic trim work gives each room a special feeling while easing transitions from window to door and from room to room. Photo taken at F on floor plan.

assortment of window sizes and heights. This approach gave me quite a bit of flexibility to select different types and sizes of windows for each room. In fact, at one point during construction, after all the windows were in place, we moved some around at the client's request.

For example, for the kitchen I planned a series of windows that would look onto the deck and lake. However, at the last minute we decided to install a small built-in bench beside the door. To give a view of the lake to anybody seated at the table, we installed a longer window there (bottom photo, facing page). The shorter windows—with higher sills—allowed room for counter space while giving a view of the lake from the kitchen sink. By varying the last window in the series, we broke away from a cookie-cutter elevation without producing a chaotic appearance.

The master-bedroom suite on the second level has plenty of cross ventilation and views on all four sides. The bathroom (left photo, facing page) and walk-in closet went on the north side, which provides privacy for the bedroom from the neighbor's house. The trees on the hill and in front of the addition produce the feeling of being in a tree house. The large expanse of windows on the south provides warmth and light and commands a spectacular view of the lake.

Curvy trim eases transitions—The two-story addition and the varied placement of windows broke up the symmetry of the basic box, so looser, less formal trim details began to make sense. We introduced curvilinear, organic shapes into the finish work to break up the hard edges of the rectangular windows and doors.

The scrolled trimwork also eased the transition between different-size windows placed next to each other. Because none of the scroll cuts is identical, each section of the trimwork has a different character (photo left).

The use of scrolled trimwork was carried through to other aspects of the finish work. In the bathroom, for example, the scrolled element became shelves and shelf brackets. In other areas, the scrollwork became a subtle transition between door trim and baseboard.

A new deck and a slew of French doors expand the living room—The existing house had a small deck that was accessible from the living room through a single door that also served as the main entrance. First, I opened the living room by adding a wall of French doors. Then I extended the deck across the front of the addition, which gave access to the deck from both the living room and the kitchen.

The deck became an extension of the living room into the terraced landscape (photo top right, facing page). Two sets of stairs—one existing and one new—now lead onto the deck, which meets the hill on one side.

As the deck was enlarged, the existing, wobbly 2x4 railings were replaced with a series of layered planters and a scrolled balustrade made from scraps of pressure-treated 1x4s. The use of balusters with organic, curvy shapes breaks up the rectilinear frame of the railing and adds an informal feeling. □

David Borenstein is an architect/builder in Red Hook, New York. Photos by Rich Ziegner.

Gaining light. The smaller footprint of the second-floor master bedroom allowed room for skylights to bring daylight to the music room. Photo taken at G on floor plan.

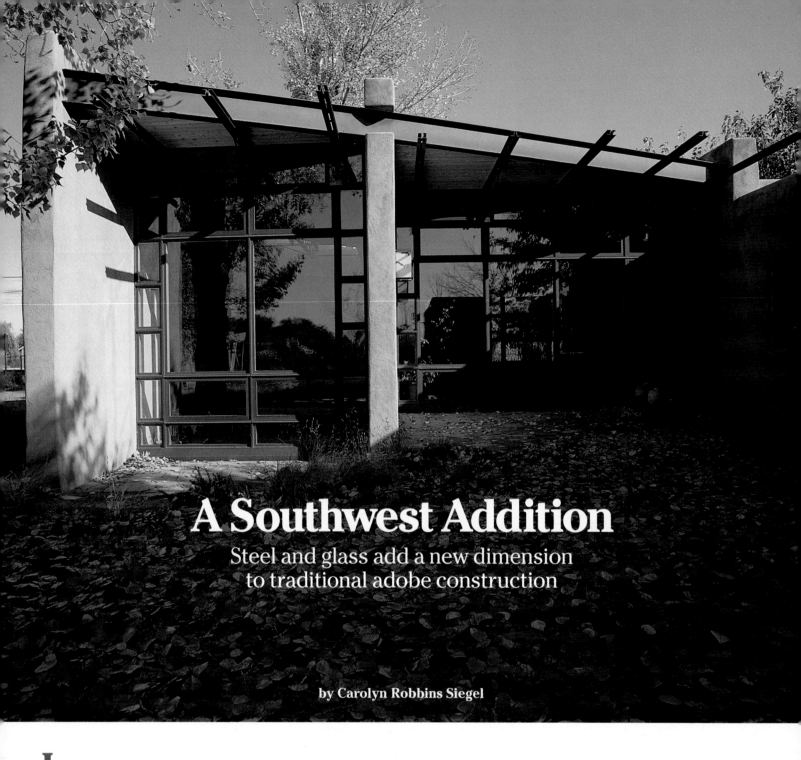

A Southwest Addition

Steel and glass add a new dimension to traditional adobe construction

by Carolyn Robbins Siegel

If it hadn't been for the six years I spent in California, I might still think of adobe houses only as the quaint boxes you find on picture postcards from the Southwest—walls of sun-cured adobe and mud mortar, and round roof beams poking through parapets at the tops of outside walls. Those are the buildings I lived in and renovated in New Mexico in the 1970s, and I grew to love their simplicity, strength and earthy shapes.

Then Santa Monica, California, intervened. That's where my husband, Jonathan Siegel, and I both studied architecture. We were influenced by the design ideas that emerged in southern California in the late 70s and early 80s. Later, we traveled to Europe and were intrigued by the manner in which new materials were combined with old building forms. When we moved to Albuquerque, New Mexico, to set up our own architectural partnership, we wanted to inject some of our new thinking into the tra-

Passive-solar design. **Two south-facing window walls let in the winter sun, but the over-hang blocks harsh summer light. The trussed joists are welded to the bottom of the steel beam above, so the window wall is nonbearing. Photo taken at A on drawing.**

ditional adobe form. We began by planning a 975-sq. ft. adobe addition to our own home, a 50-year-old house on a quiet side street.

Our plan revolved around an extensive use of steel and glass (photo above). Steel-trussed joists and cantilevered steel beams aren't standard materials for putting a roof over your head in residential adobe construction. And with that in mind we knew the project would cross typical adobe boundaries.

A large, curved adobe wall enclosing the north and west sides would provide protection from cold winds in winter and from the hot western

sun in summer (drawing facing page). On the south side, two glass walls totaling 360 sq. ft. would let in the low winter sun. The concrete floor would be warmed both by the sun and by hydronic radiant heat. On the roof, we added a south-facing clerestory to wash light down on interior walls and on a fireplace below (photo p. 98). The interior walls would be cloaked in a raw, pinkish-tan plaster, and the exterior walls would be finished in a sand-textured stucco. From footings to roof, the addition would be a meeting of regional adobe materials and contemporary technology.

After demolition, new footings—Before we could pour footings for the addition, there was the question of what to do with what was already there. The house was capped by four different roofs, and it had all the charm of a run-down chicken coop. In two days we demolished a small, badly constructed bedroom and a bathroom and cleared the way for the addition. Once the rubble had been cleared, we poured the footings and the first of two concrete slabs (a thin finish slab was poured later on top of the rough slab for the radiant heat).

The footings support four steel-reinforced columns made of concrete block, an integral part of the structural design (drawing right). The columns support load-bearing steel I-beams on the south side of the addition and at the north entry porch. To make a secure bond between the block columns and the slab, we wired sections of #6 rebar vertically to the steel that had been cast into the concrete footings and lifted the blocks over the rebar. Between every course of block, we inserted horizontal ties of #3 rebar and wired them to the vertical steel reinforcement.

While solidly linking the concrete-block columns to the slab, we also needed to tie the columns securely to the adobe walls that would butt into them. We opted for 4-in. wide strips of expanded metal lath set in the block joints every third course. The lath was embedded 6 in. through the concrete block mortar joints into the grouted core of the column, with 18 in. left to be set into the adjoining adobe mortar joints.

After the columns had been erected, and the mortar had set, we filled the columns with concrete. Because the project started in the middle of the winter, temperatures were below freezing on many nights. Frozen concrete can mean structural failure, so we protected the columns as they rose from the slab with plastic tents and portable electric heaters. It all looked pretty strange, but it worked.

Adobe goes up—The old recipe for adobe calls for clay, sand, silt and sometimes straw. Today there are two more-modern versions: semistabilized adobe, which contains 5% to 15% asphalt emulsion or portland cement; and fully stabilized adobe, which contains a higher proportion of the additive. We chose the two stabilized varieties and had 3,000 adobe blocks delivered (three-quarters of what we would need). Each block, roughly 10 in. by 14 in. by 3½ in., weighs 35 lb.

We used fully stabilized adobe blocks and a portland-cement mortar for the first two courses because we wanted the bottom of the wall to be as water resistant as possible. On the next two courses we used semistabilized adobe blocks and added an asphalt emulsion to the adobe mortar (which consists of the same material as the blocks). From there on up, it was semistabilized adobe and traditional mud mortar. We were fortunate to have the services of a skilled adobe builder, William Stoddard.

We were careful to provide a method of attachment for cabinetry, doors and windows by inserting what we call wood bucks and gringo blocks in the walls as we went. Bucks are rough 2x frames that are set in place and braced to provide window and door openings. Gringo blocks, which are standard in adobe construction, are 2x4s nailed together to form an open box with the same dimensions as an adobe block. They are set in the wall and filled with

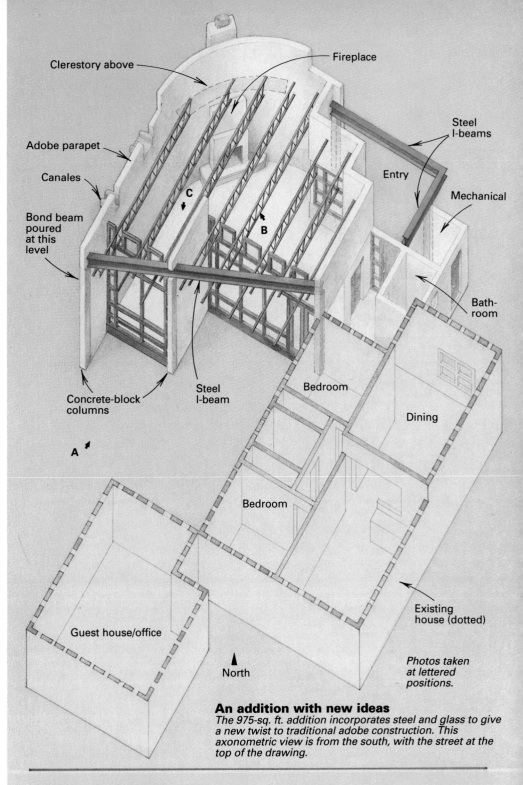

An addition with new ideas
The 975-sq. ft. addition incorporates steel and glass to give a new twist to traditional adobe construction. This axonometric view is from the south, with the street at the top of the drawing.

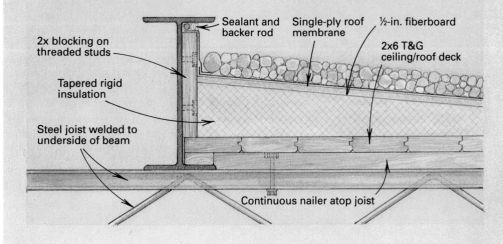

Steel-beam parapet
The steel I-beam on the south side of the addition also forms the roof parapet. The steel-trussed joists supporting the roof are welded to the bottom of the beam, freeing the window walls below from any structural weight.

A marriage of old and new. The adobe walls are traditional, but the steel isn't. A clerestory over the fireplace washes the interior wall with light. The braces running perpendicular to the joists are 1¼-in. angle iron. Photo taken from B on drawing, p. 97.

mortar to provide backing for bookshelves, baseboard and door and window frames.

We also laid underground-rated electrical cable on top of the third course of adobe blocks for outlets, and on upper courses for wall switches. Adobe walls can always be routed out later for electrical cable, but it is far easier to install wiring as you go. Leads are run out from the main cable to boxes that are set at wall surfaces (with an allowance for the finish plaster coat).

Before completing the walls, we also put up one additional column that would link the existing house with the addition. Rather than concrete block, this column would be cast concrete within an existing wall and would hold up one

end of the large steel I-beam on the south side of the addition. To make this column look less like an afterthought, we sawed through the stucco and hollow-clay tile of the existing house and made a slot for the new column. Vertical steel was set into drilled holes in the existing concrete footing, then wooden formwork was built to re-create the corner. Buckets of concrete poured into the form flowed into the adjacent empty cells of the clay tile to create a bond with the old wall.

Bond beam links adobe and steel—A concrete beam ties the house together. The beam is 10 in. wide by 8 in. high and is cast in place on

top of the adobe walls. It is connected to both the concrete-block columns and the two cantilevered steel beams on the north side of the house. The bond beam also supports the north end of the eight steel joists that hold up the roof. Getting ready for this complicated and important pour was a tense episode in the project.

The forms for the bond beam consisted of ½-in. plywood strips 12 in. wide, which are held together by 1x crosspieces on top and heavy baling wire threaded across the middle. The forms slipped down over the walls and stopped when the wire rested on top of the adobe. Shallow saw cuts, or kerfs, in the plywood forms every 4 in. let us bend them on curved wall sections. We

Using steel-trussed joists

We decided to use open web steel joists (also called steel-trussed joists) for a couple of reasons. For one, we liked the way they looked. Steel-trussed joists also are capable of spanning long distances. And steel-trussed joists weigh less than wooden beams or laminated beams capable of supporting the same load—and thus are easier to install and require less concrete foundation support.

Unlike dimensional lumber at a lumberyard, steel-trussed joists are not usually stockpiled by a supplier. That's because there is no standard length. The joists are made up after you order them, so you need to allow ample time for having them fabricated. Field modifications are difficult, if not impossible—you just can't trim them to size on site as you can with 2x stock. In short, I can't emphasize enough how important it is to consult the manufacturer's representative plus a structural engineer for any unusual designs you may be planning. Our plans, for instance, called for the joists to be welded to the bottom of a steel I-beam on the south side of the addition. This unusual means of support was thoroughly checked by our engineer.

Joist sizing and selection—A steel-joist supplier can provide catalogs with design tables and other information you need to choose the right joist for the job. We gave our supplier plans and information about roof loads, spans and connections—and the supplier sized the joists and worked out the cross-bridging details for us. We also sought the services of a structural engineer because the joists were used in an unusual way: The top chord of each joist was supported from below at one end, and from above on the other end. And we made sure we had a professional on site when it was time for the welding. It was no time for an amateur. The joists also can be bolted into place, but that must be specified when ordering.

Our steel supplier provided 16K9 joists that are 16 in. deep and ranging in length from 14 ft. to 32 ft. (The joists are installed on a curved wall; hence the different lengths.) To size the joists, multiply the depth of the joist (16 in.) by two, and you'll have that joist's maximum span in feet (32). The "K" in 16K9 is a designation from the Steel Joist Institute that indicates the design specifications of the joist. The "16" is the depth in inches; and "9" is tied into the span tables provided by the supplier.

Working with steel—The joists we used weigh 10 lb. per ft., so the longest one (32 ft.) weighed 320 lb. and cost about 38¢ per lb. It's common to use a forklift to set steel joists into place, but we used a small crane because we had other steel beams to move. The steel-trussed joist weighed less than an engineered wood beam with the same bearing capacity—and that makes it easier and safer to move the joists.

Bridging, which is cross-bracing similar to the bridging that you would install in a traditional wood-floor system, is essential to keep the joists vertical until the ceiling or roof sheathing is installed. The catalogs available from joist suppliers include tables to help you calculate the bridging. In our situation, the bridging is 1/8-in. thick steel angle (in an "L" shape), 1¼ in. on a side.

The joists were delivered with an iron oxide, oil-based primer—just the color we wanted. Steel exposed to the weather was given a finish coat of paint in the same color. Other materials were left in their raw state, too, so the joists fit right in. They could, of course, be painted any color you want. I've even heard of people having joists chromed.

For more information about steel joists, contact the Steel Joist Institute, 1205 48th Ave. North, Suite A, Myrtle Beach, S. C. 29577; (803) 449-0487. *—C. S.*

warehouse or a factory, not in an adobe dwelling. But using them to frame the roof of the addition (see sidebar, left) meant that the glass curtain walls on the south side of the addition didn't have to bear any weight from the roof. With the joists supported from above and all that glass below, the roof-ceiling plane could appear to float in space.

We ordered the joists through Vulcraft (a division of Nucor Corp., P. O. Box 186, Grapeland, Texas 75844; 409-687-4665). Because the north wall was curved, each joist was a different length and keyed to a specific position. The idea was to set the top chords of the joists on the steel plates that had been cast into the concrete on the north wall. Along the south wall, the top chords of the joists would be welded to the bottom of a 35-ft. long steel beam set atop the concrete-block columns. At 14 in. deep, however, this beam had yet another purpose: It became the parapet where roof decking, insulation and roof membrane all terminated (bottom drawing, p. 97).

The steel joists had to be parallel and align with window mullions 4 ft. o. c. that would be installed later. With a small truck-mounted crane setting the steel in place, we hung a plumb bob from the center of each joist and aligned it with a measured point on the concrete floor. The welder lined up each joist in turn 12 ft. over the floor, clamped it and then welded it to the bottom of the beam. At first our structural engineer didn't think that welded connections would be strong enough to support the roof. But after he did some calculations, he found that welded connections would be sufficient, provided that each joint between beam and joist had a minimum of 2½ in. of weld; we managed to get 14 in. of weld on each.

With the steel set, the rest of the roof deck followed. A 2x4 pine nailer was bolted along the top chord of each joist with ½-in dia. bolts 18 in. o. c. Next the 2x6 T&G decking was installed, and the exterior walls were extended above the roof in the form of traditional adobe parapets. Extra wood blocks were installed on the curved north wall over the fireplace to anchor the framing for the clerestory. Once the roof deck was installed, we cut the curved 2-ft. by 15-ft. opening for the clerestory, framed the 2x4 parapet walls above and installed double-glazed glass into site-built frames.

High-tech roof and floor—Albuquerque doesn't get much rain or snow, so roofs can have a low slope (¼ in. per ft.) and drain from scuppers that we call canales. Back when people had lots of time on their hands, the roofs of adobe houses were made of packed dirt over densely packed grasses and sticks (or latillas) that were supported by vigas, the round roof beams. Those roofs needed a lot of maintenance. Then came built-up roofs of asphalt and hot-mopped tar. But the big temperature swings and intense ultraviolet radiation here destroy asphalt roofs within seven years or so.

Frequent maintenance and replacement were a couple of traditions we didn't need. Instead, we installed an EPDM (ethylene propylene di-

---

hung wire from the 1x crosspieces at the top of the forms to keep horizontal rebar in place.

To provide a solid bearing for the steel joists, we attached 6-in. by 10-in. plates of ¼-in. steel to the beam along the north wall. The plates were nailed to additional crosspieces that were attached to the top of the forms. When the bond beam was poured, steel anchor studs on the bottom of the plates were cast into the concrete. We had to make sure that each plate was not only level but in the same plane as the others.

The two cantilevered steel beams over the street-side entry, 9 ft. and 17 ft. long, also rely on the bond beam for support. The shorter beam sits atop a block column and was cast into the

bond beam. The second beam sits in a pocket that had been made in the block column on the other side of the entry. The beams had to be perfectly aligned because the bottom flanges catch one end of the T&G ceiling in the entryway. The ceiling, in turn, had to line up with the tops of metal-clad window frames. The beams were mitered and welded at the unsupported corner, and once that steel was braced in place, the concrete for the bond beam was poured. It was a complex convergence of mud, concrete and steel. We were all relieved once it was finished.

Goodbye heavy roof timbers—Steel-trussed joists are the kind of thing you'd usually find in a

A wall of windows. The two sets of windows, each 12 ft. high, are braced by steel that's hidden inside the top casing. Small spaces around the steel joists at the tops of the windows are sealed with Lexan and caulk. Photo taken at C on drawing, p. 97.

ene monomer) single-ply membrane. It's like a giant rubber inner tube cut open and laid flat. It can be glued down, held with mechanical fasteners or fixed in place with rock ballast (ours is ballasted). We installed the membrane over expanded polystyrene (EPS) insulation that was tapered to provide slope for drainage. With an R-value of 4.17 per in., the insulation is providing R-41 at its thickest point. Between the roof membrane and the insulation is ½-in. fiberboard that protects the insulation from the heavy rock ballast above.

For heating the addition we chose a hydronic radiant floor system. On top of the slab we had poured earlier, the mechanical subcontractor laid 1 in. of rigid perforated EPS insulation, welded wire mesh and then an In-Floor polybutylene tubing system (Gypcrete Corp., 920 Hamel Road, Hamel, Minn. 55340; 800-356-7887). While the concrete was still workable, the contractor tooled ½-in. deep expansion joints to minimize cracking. Unfortunately, we didn't take the advice of the contractor when he suggested two additional expansion joints at wall corners. We didn't want the additional joints because they didn't fit the rectangular pattern in the rest of the floor. Sure enough, that's where

cracks appeared. The expansion joints were later filled with colored tile grout, and the floor was sealed with clear mop-on wax.

Installing windows and wall finishes—The windows we picked are double-glazed, insulated metal-clad wood units (Eagle Window and Door, 375 East 9th St., Dubuque, Iowa 52004; 319-556-2270). The larger window unit spans more than 18 ft. and rises almost 12 ft. from floor to ceiling (photo above). Because Albuquerque can have 70 mph winds from the southwest in the spring, we added ¼-in. by 6-in. horizontal steel braces to the two window openings. The steel, laid flat and attached to nailers in the walls, resists lateral forces. We also had to fill some odd-shaped spaces above the window units where the steel joists poke through the south wall. We cut pieces of ¼-in. thick Lexan, made slots for the steel joists and then sealed the remaining gaps with a clear silicone caulk.

The exterior of the building is a straightforward three-coat stucco over a spray foam insulation polyurethane that was required by city building codes. For the inside of the house, we hired a plaster crew to apply a three-coat plaster finish. We used Structo-Lite plaster (U. S. Gypsum, 14643

Dallas Parkway, Dallas, Texas 75240; 214-490-0771) because it has a natural pinkish-tan color and needs no painting or color additives. To guard against an uneven appearance, the crew plastered each wall area to corners and window edges without a break. But that attention to detail is what produced a uniform plaster surface. The softly mottled walls invite people to brush their hands across it. After a two-week curing period, we applied a clear acrylic resin sealer to the wall with a spray bottle and rubbed it in with a lambswool mitt (OKON W-1 Waterproofing Sealer, OKON, Inc., 6000 West 13th Ave., Lakewood, Colo. 80214; 303-232-3571). The finish prevents stains from sinking into the plaster.

The finish details that usually make up the last stage of a construction project were minimal in our case. Although we did have to clean a little plaster off the wood ceiling and the floor, there was no drywall to tape, texture and paint, no trim that needed painting, and no carpet or tile that had to be set. The raw finish materials speak for themselves. ☐

Carolyn Robbins Siegel and Jonathan Siegel are partners in Siegel Design, an architectural firm in Albuquerque, N. M. Photos by Scott Gibson.

A Well-Lit Addition

A glazed cupola and exterior transoms let daylight into a new family room with northern exposure

by Robert L. Marx

Often, the challenge of renovation is finding the solution that provides for the clients' new needs while preserving what they enjoy in their home. This project introduced an ironic twist, for the home's most distinctive elements also contributed to its shortcoming.

The dilemma—My clients loved their home, especially for its ivy-covered fieldstone walls and its arched windows. An old estate carriage house in Greenwich, Connecticut, the building had been carefully converted into a residence. Al-

though the layout of the first floor made the best of three arched windows on the west elevation, the rooms on the first floor were dark. My goal was to expand the house and to brighten the interior. However, the plan made expansion impossible without disturbing the fieldstone walls, and the owners wanted to leave both the walls and the arched windows intact.

So I decided to add living space at the back of the house (photo p. 103). I connected the addition to the house by removing an earlier addition that contained two small, unused rooms.

Doing away with the old addition increased the area available for new construction and provided a direct connection between the new family room and the rest of the house. More importantly, it preserved the old stone walls.

However, the addition's northern exposure does not provide the most advantageous solar orientation, so I had to search for ways to capture natural light.

Reaching for the light—Because I was using a combination of glass doors, transoms and over-

Section of roof framing

Within the gable roof, two headers support the cupola; these headers are fastened to doubled rafters at each end of the cupola. A tripled header carries the cripple rafters at the shed-dormer opening. This header is fastened with bolts and clip angles to tripled rafters on each side of the door alcove. At the top of the alcove opening, the lower transom header hangs from a pair of wood 2xs that are bolted to the tripled rafters; this header is concealed in the soffit inside the room.

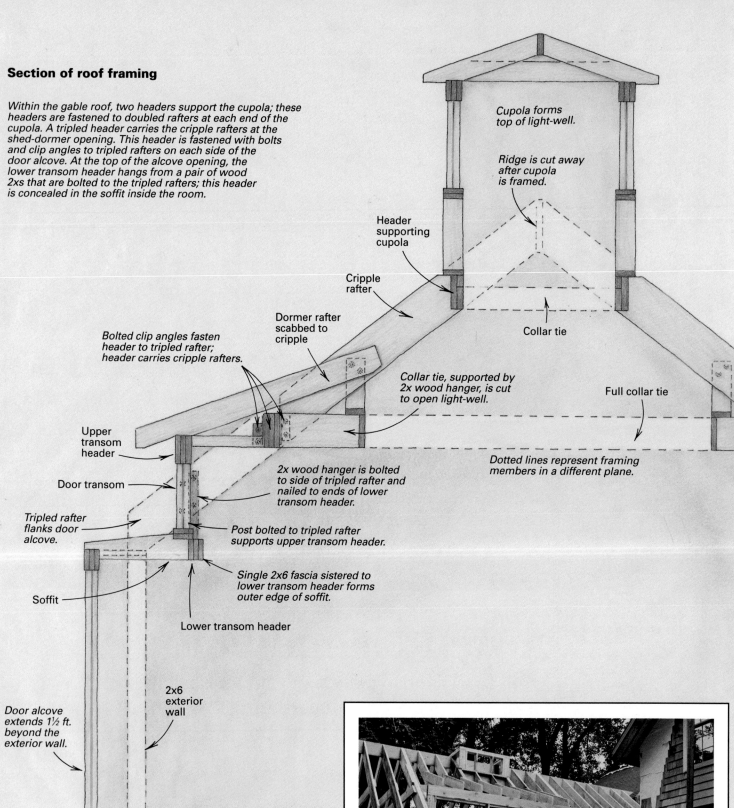

Cupola forms top of light-well.

Ridge is cut away after cupola is framed.

Header supporting cupola

Cripple rafter

Dormer rafter scabbed to cripple

Collar tie

Bolted clip angles fasten header to tripled rafter; header carries cripple rafters.

Collar tie, supported by 2x wood hanger, is cut to open light-well.

Full collar tie

Upper transom header

2x wood hanger is bolted to side of tripled rafter and nailed to ends of lower transom header.

Dotted lines represent framing members in a different plane.

Door transom

Tripled rafter flanks door alcove.

Post bolted to tripled rafter supports upper transom header.

Single 2x6 fascia sistered to lower transom header forms outer edge of soffit.

Soffit

Lower transom header

Door alcove extends 1½ ft. beyond the exterior wall.

2x6 exterior wall

Framing the openings. The door alcove is bumped out 1½ ft. to match the thickness of the old stone wall. The door transom has a shed roof.

head glazing to light the addition, my goal was to arrange the glazing into a composition in keeping with the house.

The windows and the doors are similar to those of the original house not only stylistically but also in how they were installed. On the interior of the original house, the thickness of the fieldstone walls is apparent because windows and doors are set deep in their openings. I wanted the addition to have the same character, even though the new walls would be framed with 2x6s. To simulate the thickness of a stone wall in the addition, the triple window and door units project 1½ ft. beyond adjacent wall planes, creating a bay window and a door alcove. Both of these projections have flat roofs. Each flat roof is lined with a lead-coated copper pan drained with scuppers.

Although 1½-ft. deep window and door openings help unify the original house and the addition, the bay window and the door alcove reduce the amount of daylight coming into the room. To overcome this loss of light, transoms were installed in the same plane as the framed walls. The window transom is framed in the gable-end wall. The door transom forms a shed dormer rising from the main roof.

Even with the transoms, the lighting was inadequate, so I concentrated next on the roof. The owners and I thought that skylights would detract from the character of the old carriage house. We all agreed that a glazed cupola would contribute more to the character of the house. The cupola, placed at the center of the ridge, lends warmth to the new family room by transmitting diffuse overhead light (photo p. 101).

The French correction—Like the windows of the original house, the new ones are double-hung wood with true divided lites (Marvin Windows, Warroad, Minn. 56763; 800-346-5128). The lite pattern of the French doors on the west elevation matches that of the windows.

I prefer the feel and the operation of French doors over sliding doors. However, manufacturers have standardized the width of French-door stiles at more than 4½ in. I planned to group three doors together and thought these stiles would look heavy. With narrow backset mortise locks easily available (Baldwin Hardware, 841 East Wyomissing Blvd., Reading, Pa. 19611; 215-777-7811), other door-sash dimensions are possible.

We had narrow-profile doors with thick sections custom built by the Woodstone Company (P. O. Box 223, Westminster, Vt. 05158; 802-722-4784). These 2-in. thick doors have 3½-in. wide stiles, which approaches the slenderness of sliding-door frames and is particularly appealing when several doors are used in combination. Like the windows, the doors are single glazed with true divided lites. With their storm panels in place, the doors provide an R-value equal to doors with ½-in. double glazing. Only the center door is operable; the others are fixed.

I sometimes use laminated glass, as I did here, rather than tempered glass where safety glazing is required by code. In larger sheets, laminated glass doesn't reflect wavy images as tempered glass sometimes does.

Headers abound in the roof—Like the roof of the old house, the new roof is a gable. But its framing was complicated by both the cupola and the shed dormer for the door transom. Tripled rafters on both sides of the door alcove carry the header for the shed dormer (photo and drawing p. 102), which is fastened with clip angles and bolts. Doubled rafters support headers that carry the cupola. Once the cupola was framed, a 42-in. section of the ridge beam was cut between the doubled rafters to open the light-well below the cupola.

The remaining rafters are single 2x12s. Their collar ties create a flat ceiling plane 10 ft. above the floor. In the center of the ceiling, there's a 7-ft. opening for the light-well. The walls of this opening are flared, with the east and west walls of the opening formed by the underside of the rafters. The north and south walls of this well are supported by headers framed on the collar ties of the tripled rafters. These walls are sloped to match the angle of the rafters, creating a symmetrical, flared light-well.

A soffit runs along the east and west walls. The plane of the bottom of the rafters is visible above this soffit. The soffit provides a smooth transition from the door transom to the roof framing and gives an intimate scale to the room.

Trim inside and out—I unified the various elements of the room—the soffits, the light-well, the window seat and the door alcove—with a picture rail. This trim runs continuously around the room, along the bottom edge of the soffit and between the transoms and the doors and the windows, forming the top casing of the doors and the windows.

The 2x12 rafters provide ample room for R-30 batt insulation and a 2-in. airspace to ventilate the underside of the roof deck. But neither the depth of the framing nor its spacing match that of the original house. The house reveals its 2x6 rafter tails and T&G bead-board roof decking at the eaves behind a 2x6 fascia board. The addition is also detailed with 2x6 rafter tails placed to match the spacing of those on the house. Within the roof framing, the inboard ends of the 2x6s are nailed into blocking that spans between the rafters. The 2x6s bear on another row of blocking along the top plate, resulting in cantilevered dummy rafter tails on the addition that match the exposed rafter tails on the main house.

Let the stone show—Details sometimes go unnoticed when they work well. One example is where the addition roof butts into the stone wall of the original house. The easiest solution to this detail—in fact, the one that had been used on another part of the house—would have been to extend the shingle siding down from the second floor over the stone on furring strips until it met the lower roofline. The sidewall flashing could then be turned up behind these shingles. But we didn't want to cover up the stone wall and didn't have to, thanks to the skill of builder Wayne Dudley of Weston, Connecticut. Dudley cut a continuous groove, or reglet, directly into the stone to flash this roof-to-wall intersection. He used an abrasive sawblade to cut the 1½-in. deep groove. Lead-coated copper flashing is held in the groove with shims and is finished with a bead of sealant. This subtle, clean detail allowed us to expose the fieldstone wall to the east and as it turns the corner. □

Robert L. Marx is an architect in Stratford, Conn. Photos by the author except where noted.

Solving two problems. **Locating the addition on the north end of the house left the fieldstone walls of the original house intact. Combining triple French doors, triple window units—both of which are topped by transoms—and a glazed cupola tastefully illuminates the new room.**

There's an awkwardness about the so-called sunroom additions typically stuck onto houses these days. These additions are usually factory-made greenhouses either with hipped or curved glazing that gives a house that certain fast-food-restaurant look. Most sunrooms don't relate to the houses they're attached to and have little or no identity. So when my clients approached me with the idea of transforming an existing screened porch into a year-round sunroom, I wanted to design a space that looked as if it had always been part of the existing house.

Columns allow for large windows—The house sits on a small knoll that is approached from below with the house angled toward the street to provide access to a gable-end basement garage. The sunroom was to be built off the corner of the house just above the garage, making the sunroom a highly visible part of the house's most prominent facade. It was imperative that the sunroom's design complement the architectural qualities of the house.

I modeled my design on the sunrooms and greenhouses found in many grand period hous-es with classical origins built in this country be-fore World War II. The open spaces between the columns supporting the roofs of these structures naturally lend themselves to considerable window area. The roof glazing could be limited without losing the open feeling. My challenge was to design an aesthetically pleasing room with large areas of glass, but one that would be comfortable and energy-efficient year-round (photo above). A deck built into the corner formed by the house and the sunroom would extend the sunroom spaces to the outdoors dur-ing the warmest months.

Once I'd resolved to use the column or pilaster as an organizing element, I quickly sorted through my basic options as to how many columns there would be on each side, whether they would be equally spaced and so on. In the interest of budget, we decided early on to use standard-size windows and to design around those dimensions. We chose Pella windows (102 Main St., Pella, Iowa 50219; 800-547-3552), which had the proportions I wanted as well as a low-maintenance factory-painted aluminum ex-terior cladding. The aluminum-clad windows al-so have a thin exterior casing that worked well with my custom exterior trim.

Instead of the large expanses of roof glazing that most sunrooms sport, I opted for a well-insulated roof with a few large skylights. These skylights allow for a visual connection to the trees and sky outside, and limiting the overhead glazing helps to keep the room from frying in the summer and freezing in the winter. The sky-lights have electronically controlled blinds and motorized openers that also help to control the room's climate.

Invisible timber connectors hold the truss-es together—I had a couple of areas of con-cern regarding the structure of the sunroom. First, because of the large amount of wall area taken up by windows, I worried about the hori-zontal shear strength of the walls. To solve this problem, I made the plywood sheathing contin-uous from the area below each window to the small sections between the windows. The nat-ural tendency in this case would have been to cover these areas with separates strips of ply-wood. To achieve the required shear strength,

A Classic Sunroom

Carefully proportioned use of flat boards, stock moldings and standard windows helps to create a space for all seasons

by Steven Gerber

the nails had to be spaced more closely together at the edges of the plywood, especially on the gable-end wall, which doesn't benefit from being attached directly to the house for any sort of lateral strength.

Another even more challenging problem was creating a roof structure for the cathedral ceiling. Because the roof framing would be fully exposed inside the sunroom, I decided to support the roof with timber trusses. The problem was how to connect the members.

I looked at several connection options, including mortise-and-tenon joints, metal plates with through bolts and metal connectors. Even though the trusses were made of 6x6 Douglas fir, I worried that a mortise-and-tenon joint wouldn't leave enough meat on the end of the horizontal member to resist the outward thrust of the roof. Plates and through bolts are clunky

Classic exterior, relaxed interior. Built-up panels and moldings create a formal facade (photo above) while exposed trusses and a wood ceiling make the interior inviting (photo right).

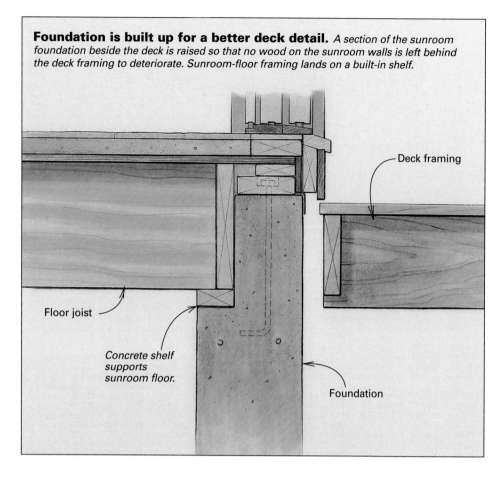

Foundation is built up for a better deck detail. *A section of the sunroom foundation beside the deck is raised so that no wood on the sunroom walls is left behind the deck framing to deteriorate. Sunroom-floor framing lands on a built-in shelf.*

Deck framing

Floor joist

Concrete shelf
supports
sunroom floor.

Foundation

and wouldn't be in character with the sunroom's interior, so I decided to use timber connectors to join the trusses.

I ended up having the roof trusses made by Green Mountain Precision Frames (P. O. Box 293, Windsor, Vt. 05089; 802-674-6145). They prefabricated the four roof trusses using their Timberlok Joinery System, a concealed, practically invisible steel-connection system.

An informal interior—I wanted the sunroom's interior to have a less formal feel than its classical exterior, so I began at the top with a natural-wood ceiling (bottom photo, p. 105). If we had sheathed the roof with standard plywood, the spacing of the roof trusses would have required additional purlins. So I used 2x6 tongue-and-groove Douglas fir instead. The 2x6 boards easily spanned the distance between the trusses, and they added beautiful color and texture to the ceiling at the same time.

To complete the roof, the Doug fir was covered with an air barrier, a 4-in. layer of foil-faced foam insulation, 2x2 furring strips (to create a ventilation cavity) and plywood sheathing. The plywood was topped with self-adhesive rubberized membrane and finally a layer of asphalt shingles. I decided to forgo the usual ridge vent for aesthetic reasons. Continuous soffit vents, a low slope (3-in-12) and good crosswinds have

kept the roof dry through the extremes of the past two New England winters.

As a counterpoint to the natural wood above, I decided to go with a stone floor. I chose an Indian slate for its deep silvery-blue color and natural cleft finish. In addition, the slate feels cool in the summer and stores heat during sunny winter days. The ½-in. thick pieces of slate were set into a 1½-in. mud bed on top of the ¾-in. plywood subfloor. The mud bed let me use larger pieces of stone and added to the thermal mass of the floor.

Exterior panels made in layers—The most enjoyable part of the project was detailing the exterior trim. For cost reasons I opted for moldings that could be made on site. I specified redwood for most of the exterior trim because redwood resists decay and holds a paint finish.

Mark Iverson of Jolin Construction in Dedham, Massachusetts, made the flat panels below each of the windows out of medium-density overlay board. He applied layers of trim on top of the board to create the recessed panel (photo bottom right, facing page). The pilasters between the windows were given a similar treatment. All critical joints in the trim were biscuit-joined to ensure that they would not open. All the trim on the outside corners of the sunroom was mitered and glued to provide a seamless, solid

appearance, and I made sure that all the trim was back-primed before it was installed.

I had hoped to put copper gutters and downspouts on the sunroom, but I found that the cost was exorbitant. The standard aluminum gutters that I looked at were out of proportion with the room. So instead I chose a less expensive PVC-gutter system made by Plastmo (8246 Sandy Court B, Jessup, Md. 20974; 800-899-0992) that was beautifully designed and just the right size (photo top right, facing page).

The small round window on the pediment was the only custom window in the sunroom. The 7-in. radius was not a size made by any of the major manufacturers, so I had it fabricated at a local shop. The round window adds a finishing touch to the facade and creates a special light feature in the interior as well.

Creative detailing means a longer-lasting deck—I designed the adjoining deck to complement the sunroom and to extend its spaces outdoors. The deck is supported by 4x4 pressure-treated posts topped with a decorative cap and wrapped in painted redwood above the deck boards. The railing pickets are all mortised into the top and bottom rails, which are attached to the posts with concealed metal angles and screws.

A redwood lattice skirt wraps around the deck to create a more finished look and to keep leaves and debris from blowing underneath. One of the lattice panels is hinged for access to the crawlspace under the deck. Another crawlspace under the sunroom is also accessible through a removable louvered panel in the foundation wall of the sunroom.

Typically, when a deck is built, sheathing or siding on the adjoining side of the house is often trapped behind the framing of the deck. This wood can't be repainted or inspected for rot without removing part of the deck. I stepped the sunroom foundation so that there is only concrete behind the deck frame (drawing above left). The sunroom's floor joists rest on a shelf that is formed on the inside of the stepped wall. This detail puts all of the painted surfaces above the deck.

The deck framing doesn't actually touch the sunroom foundation wall. But along the existing wall of the house, where the deck joists are supported, I removed the painted clapboards that would have been concealed behind the rim joist and had aluminum flashing wrapped over the top of the joist. I also left a small ⅛-in. gap between the stained surfaces and the painted surfaces. The gap makes it easier to paint and repaint without leaving a sloppy edge. □

Steven Gerber is an architect based in Brookline, Massachusetts. Photos by Roe A. Osborn.

Drawing: Dan Thornton

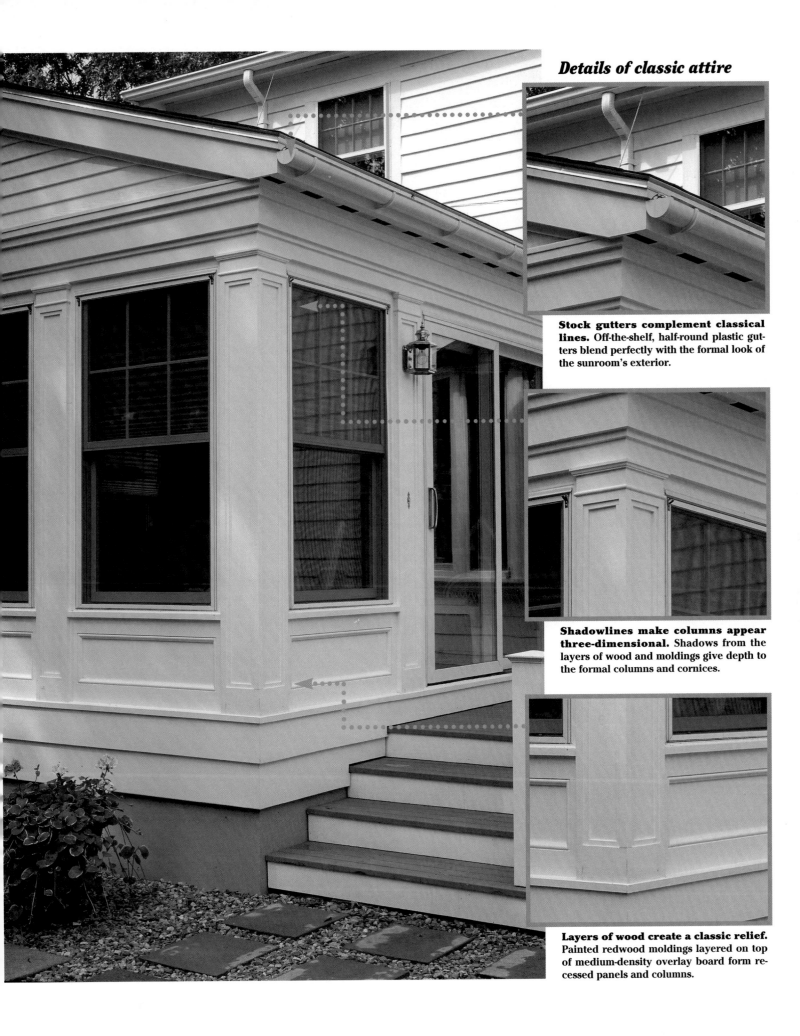

Details of classic attire

Stock gutters complement classical lines. Off-the-shelf, half-round plastic gutters blend perfectly with the formal look of the sunroom's exterior.

Shadowlines make columns appear three-dimensional. Shadows from the layers of wood and moldings give depth to the formal columns and cornices.

Layers of wood create a classic relief. Painted redwood moldings layered on top of medium-density overlay board form recessed panels and columns.

A Tiny English Kitchen

Contrasting materials and colors along with
freestanding cabinetry add charm to
this London studio kitchen

by John Ferro Sims

In the late 1920s noted sculptor Henry Moore moved to 11A Parkhill Road in London and used the main room as his studio. Later in the 30s, the group of artists living in the area, including Moore and the abstract artist Piet Mondrian, became known as the Parkhill Road group. Moore remained here until some houses on the street were damaged by German bombs during World War II. When I acquired the property in 1971, it was still a "studio with rooms" on the tax lists, a rather prosaic description for a flat with such a history.

My overriding concern when renovating this studio and its kitchen was to maintain the special atmosphere that had attracted Moore in the first place. Huge windows overlook a garden at the back, and the summer foliage conceals the fact that the studio is only five minutes from the center of London.

I didn't want the kitchen to compete visually with the rest of the studio, but I did want it to reflect my eclectic tastes (photo right). Colors and textures are important to me, and while I was unsure initially what woods to use for cabinets and trim, I knew they had to have strong visual impact. They also needed to work well with the old reddish-brown pitch-pine wood floor and with the different surfaces I wanted to use, such as granite, sandblasted glass and stainless steel. Finding the right cabinetmaker/designer to help with the project could have been a problem. Fortunately, I met Big Egg.

After leaving school at 15 to become an apprentice chair maker, Egbert Sullivan progressed to an apprenticeship at Heals, the famous London furniture store. Egg established Big Egg Designs in 1980 after he spent two years

at the London College of Furniture, a spell as a kitchen fitter in Leeds and a stint as an antique-furniture restorer.

Egg's basic philosophy is simple: Good design needn't be expensive, yet no matter how exciting a design may appear, it is useless if drawers stick or if function is sacrificed. Egg's vivacious, modern approach to furniture-making and his understanding of the visual impact of interesting design made him the perfect collaborator on this project.

A walnut counter is at the heart of the kitchen—The main work counter is the functional and visual focal point of a kitchen, and for this I chose American walnut. The wood is kind to cutlery and crockery, and I admire its deep, rich color and its variable grain.

I wanted a work surface that would be wider and thicker than standard; mine is 110 in. long, including the sink, 29 in. wide and 1¾ in. thick. Walnut is a stable wood little affected by heat or humidity, particularly when it is this thick. Small marks blend easily into the dark color and grain structure, and moisture marks disappear quickly. Every year or two, I scour the surface with an ordinary kitchen-pan scrub and then vigorously rub tung oil or olive oil with the grain. Afterward, I wipe off the excess oil and let it slowly dry for about a day. This treatment clears up discolorations and knife marks, and it leaves the counter looking clean and fresh.

Big Egg suggested incorporating the 10-in. deep Belfast, or butler's, sink to accommodate my need for a large washing-up bowl and to eliminate the need for a big dishwasher. The white sink also provides a contrasting color and

material to the walnut work area. A small refrigerator and a compact dishwasher are hidden behind the paneled doors beneath the countertop. On each side of the sink, drainage grooves routed into the work counter channel water safely toward the drain.

Egg suggested using maple for the cabinet-door stiles and rails, with panels of contrasting walnut veneers. All the carcase work is of medium-density fiberboard (MDF), an economical and stylish material when properly finished. Like all the woodwork, the MDF was sealed with

Sandblasted-glass panels emphasize the cupboards, not the contents. The tall window and even taller ceiling allow room for this high cupboard. A compact refrigerator and a small dishwasher are concealed behind the walnut-paneled doors beneath the counter and to the left of the extra-deep single-bowl sink.

lacquer and rubbed with steel wool, then buffed to a finish with clear wax and a soft cloth.

Egg suggested that the five-burner stove, or hob as we call it in England, and oversize oven be placed under the stairs and out of direct sight of the dining table and seating area. He also knew the hob would work best at a height of 30 in. rather than the standard 36 in. off the floor. The hob is set in granite, and the backsplash and sides are covered in stainless steel. A maple board tops the stainless-steel backsplash and carries the kitchen-implement rail.

Custom cabinetry makes the most of a limited space—Below the stairs to the right of the hob/oven unit is a cabinet of large drawers. The three top drawers measure 25 in. long by 20 in. wide by 5½ in. deep and provide plenty of room for cutlery, additional cooking utensils and miscellaneous kitchen items. The 11½-in. deep bottom drawer provides bigger storage for dry goods in larger containers, such as pasta and rice. These drawers are set on heavy-duty double-extension slides for strength and are compartmentalized for both maximum use and efficiency. The knobs, all turned by Big Egg in both maple and walnut, were used either to match or to contrast with the drawer faces. The 36-in. high maple-and-walnut counter above these drawers is 34 in. deep by 24 in. wide and is designed to fit slightly recessed under the 36-in. wide stairs.

To the left of the hob is a corner cupboard with a double-hinged door for pots and pans. Above the hob and to the left are tall, nonstandard storage cupboards. They open right to left for easier access, though Egg's assistant, Sally, didn't notice this and assumed they opened conventionally when she was drilling holes for the knobs. She nearly fainted when she discovered she had drilled a hole on the wrong side of one door. Although we forgave her, the hole remains.

It was important to maximize the available odd-shaped space, so Egg built cupboards of varying sizes and shapes to fit the triangular area below the stairs. The space between the window and the return wall limited the depth of these cupboards to 12 in. Because the cupboards aren't seen from the sitting area, it wasn't important that they look like independent pieces of furniture like the more visible and larger glass-paneled unit on the adjacent wall. The cabinet directly above the hob contains a retractable five-speed ventilation hood with a built-in light.

At the base of both the oven and the drawer unit where the toe-kick is normally placed are additional drawers (photo facing page) with finger holes instead of knobs. In fact, wherever there was available space, we opted to take it for usable storage.

The 5-ft. tall cupboard above and to the left of the sink is quite slim, only 9 in. deep, and has glass panels that are sandblasted nearly three-quarters of their length (photo p. 109). This leaves the upper two shelf depths with clear glass. Two low-voltage lights are set inside these cupboards, and two are underneath and directed toward the work surface. Another low-voltage pair are mounted beneath the hob-side cupboard.

The design of the cupboard above the main work counter needed to harmonize with the entrance door to the left, the large window to the right and the tall ceiling. The cupboard's 9-in. depth was determined by the size of the items that would be stored in it—coffee, tea, jars and bottles containing olive oil and vinegar—and by the need for it to protrude over the work counter as little as possible.

Because the cupboard can easily be seen from the other end of the studio room more than 20 ft. away, I thought it important that it appear as a free-hanging unit and not built in like the cupboards over the hob. The cupboard looks substantial with its pediment cap, but it also appears light because of its maple construction, glass

Kitchen furniture. Tucked into an alcove, the dresser displays and stores the author's colorful crockery. Bird's-eye maple provides subtle contrast to the walnut-paneled doors in the rest of the kitchen.

A convenient storage alcove. Lacquered, waxed MDF is an economical choice for cabinets and shelves. The countertop above the radiator matches the granite details elsewhere in the kitchen.

panels and interior lighting. The upper and lower cabinets are linked visually by a high granite backsplash. Besides matching the granite under the hob and in the alcove to the left of the entrance door, this panel adds a different texture and color to the composition, and it contrasts the wood.

A freestanding dresser provides stylish storage—It was clear that the space available in the immediate kitchen area would never be

sufficient to contain the crockery. Additionally, I wished to display my modest collection of modern plates acquired over the years from Italy and Spain. A new dresser loosely based on a much smaller Victorian oak dresser sitting at the opposite wall of the room solved the problem of storage and helped to link the kitchen with the rest of the studio (top photo).

After Egg showed me a range of wood samples, it was clear that the blond color of American maple would allow my plate collection to

Making the most of limited space. Situated in the awkward triangle under the stairs, a cabinet of large and sturdy drawers provides useful storage for utensils and dry goods. Drawers are also located in the normally unused toe-kick area under both the cabinet and the stove.

stand out well. The size of the dresser was mainly dictated by the width of the space into which it had to fit and by carefully ensuring that the heights of all the cabinetry were different. It is 7 ft. 9 in. high, 6 ft. 6 in. long, and it has a maximum depth of 21 in. Egg designed the turned legs and the spindles that subdivide the top shelf, and I suggested that the lower cupboard doors should be made to look like double drawers. The wonderfully subtle color and texture of the bird's-eye maple veneer for the top cup-

board panels really finishes off the dresser in a marvelous way.

Between the dresser and the entrance door is a built-in cabinet of painted MDF (bottom photo, facing page). Underneath the matching granite shelf is a radiator, and shelves above provide storage for jugs, glassware and other small items. The electrical panel is also hidden here. □

John Ferro Sims is a photographer living in London, England. Photos by the author.

A Stylish, Functional Kitchen

Spare, elegant detailing in plaster, concrete and wood distinguishes this contemporary kitchen

by Fu Tung Cheng

It is always challenging to bring a modern aesthetic to an existing home. When Jean Krois and Howard Hertz of Berkeley, California, asked me to remodel the kitchen of their Spanish-style house, I knew it would be a delicate balancing act. They are fashion designers, and as such have very refined tastes.

Our firm specializes in contemporary designs, but their house epitomizes the mellow patina of 1940s California Spanish vernacular. It has oversize beams, thick plaster walls, wrought iron and earthy tile, all of which contribute to a sense of well-being and security. Our plan was to use these same materials in the new kitchen, but with a contemporary edge.

Our first order of business was to evaluate the bar p. 114). We decided to add a narrow strip of bar p. 62). We decided to add a narrow strip of floor space to the kitchen. Builder Craig Reese of Indian Rock Construction began this expansion work and the removal of the original walls, and we refined the various details that would stitch the expanded space into a cohesive room.

Concrete finishes at hand and underfoot—
At the opening to the kitchen, two steps up from the front entry, a concrete floor merges with a concrete cabinet base and the maple floor that covers most of the room (photo right). This concrete entry slab is built atop a wooden subfloor, and it is a mere ⁷⁄₈ in. thick. To keep it from cracking, we reinforced the slab with Laticrete Pro-Float lath, a plastic mesh typically used for strengthening mortar beds for tilework (Laticrete; 800-243-4788). Although somewhat expensive, we've found that it prevents the hairline cracking endemic in thin slabs. We far prefer Pro-Float lath to polypropylene fiber reinforcing, which tends to appear on the surface during finishing.

We darkened the color of the entry slab with a 2% carbon-black integral cement color (2 lb. of pigment per 100 lb. of cement). For a small job such as this one, we prepare the concrete on site, using a six-sack mix. The base under the cabinets is an equivalent mix, with ultramarine blue pigment added to the carbon black. Con-

Sculpture meets kitchen. Above the concrete apron, a sleek pantry in vertical-grain Douglas fir stands at the entry to the kitchen. The trapezoidal panels are doors above, drawers below. A 2-in. thick poplar counter edged with natural cypress sits atop the base cabinets. The minimalist shelves extending over the counter are ¼-in. steel. Photo taken at A on floor plan.

This concrete counter is sloped for drainage. Brass inlays cast into the sink-counter drain board protect the concrete from heavy abrasion and provide runners for the chopping block, and they elevate pots, pans and dishware for better drying. Photo taken at B on floor plan.

crete countertops are one of our signature details. The counter in this kitchen includes a recessed drain board with brass runners and a wooden chopping block that slides along the runners (photo p. 113).

We cast the counters, which are at least 3 in. to 4 in. thick, upside down in our shop in wooden molds that are lined with polyethylene or Mylar. Blocks for the tapered drain boards, elevation changes and sink knockouts are shaped into the molds. Before the counter is cast, we center $\frac{1}{2}$-in. rebar a couple of inches from the edges and on 12-in. centers throughout the mold. We use a seven-sack mix with expanded shale aggregate to make the counters. The shale is lighter than typical aggregate and gets the weight down to about 100 lb. per cu. ft.

Precise agitation with a vibrator is necessary to articulate the fine detail in the mold. As the concrete cures, we make sure the temperature stays above 50°F, and we control moisture evaporation to ensure proper curing.

Concrete counters need to be sealed, and the need for sealing is the counters' one potential weakness. Topical sealers such as epoxies, urethanes and water-based acrylic copolymers prevent staining, but they leave a glossy layer that detracts from the concrete. Penetrating sealers, which typically contain silicone, don't interfere with the concrete's rich color and texture. But they have to be renewed from time to time, and penetrating sealers can't prevent staining. To my eye, this staining simply enhances the beauty of the concrete, much the way wear and tear on a wood counter creates a patina over the years.

Hefty cabinets under the counter—For supporting concrete countertops, we insist on cabinets made from furniture-grade plywood carcases. Cabinets made from particleboard just aren't sturdy enough. We specify cabinets with vertical panels no farther than 24 in. apart, and we make them with double layers of $\frac{3}{4}$-in. plywood. We also apply $\frac{3}{4}$-in. plywood backs to these cabinets, along with a full $\frac{3}{4}$-in. plywood top. The cabinets sit atop bases that correspond to the vertical panels and the carcase perimeters, which ensures direct transfer of the weight of the counter to the floor framing. If necessary, we reinforce the floor to make sure it's strong enough to take the weight. On longer counters, the mold is sectioned into two or three pieces. These breaks are over verticals in the cabinets to ensure proper bearing under counter edges.

Sometimes our cabinets include vertical concrete elements. For example, in this kitchen, the concrete apron at the entry to the kitchen flows up the side of a cabinet that embraces a small coffee-prep counter (photo top left, facing page). Like the other cabinets in this kitchen, the coffee center was made by Guba/Craig

Changing the floor plan

In the original floor plan, the living room was grand in scale, and the kitchen and dining areas were relatively small (top floor plan below). We drew up a measured plan of the existing conditions and studied it to visualize how people moved through the spaces. We like to start from this overview rather than from the clients' initial wish list. Often, clients have long suffered with inconveniences and details they would like to change that are too specific to serve as points of departure for devising a new plan. For example, the clients might want cabinets in a type of wood they have longed for, or perhaps a window with a view, or a door to a deck, or a breakfast nook. We dutifully note all of these desires, then set them aside for the time being while we approach the floor plan with a fresh outlook. We consider all possibilities within some reasonable outer limits of the budget. Then we narrow down the options and try to incorporate the specific requirements.

Initially, Howard and Jean wanted to engage the kitchen and dining area with the front yard, provide room for a washer and dryer, increase storage and create more openness from the kitchen-prep area to the dining area. We came up with three scenarios: one that linked the kitchen to the front yard, one that separated the dining and cooking areas and one that was a farmhouse-style layout centering all of the action around the dining table.

Howard and Jean chose the last scenario (bottom floor plan below), which required that we gain a precious 50-sq. ft. strip along the kitchen's west wall to accommodate the sink and its counter.—*F. T. C.*

Take out one wall, move another. *Bisected by a partition, the original kitchen and dining room were isolated from one another and felt skimpy in a house of otherwise generous rooms. The new plan joined the two spaces into one and moved the west wall out 3 ft., gaining room for a stacking washer and dryer next to the refrigerator.*

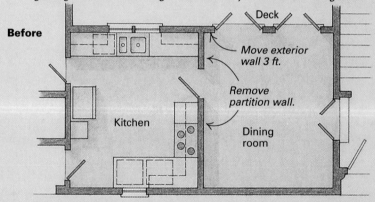

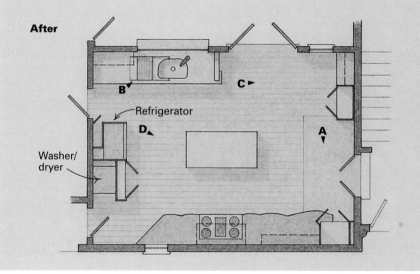

Corner counter devoted to coffee. Bluish-gray concrete slabs add counterpoint to this geometric composition in honey-colored fir. Note how the change in grain direction adds a subtle touch to the coloration. Opening a door reveals the dyed block of bird's-eye maple that completes the door pull (photo below). Photos taken at C on floor plan.

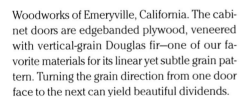

A country kitchen with an uptown soul. Flanked by the dining table, the stove counter stretches along a wall of coral-colored plaster. A range hood lined with stainless steel folds outward over the stove. The hood's three coats of plaster are strengthened by expanded-metal lath welded to its angle-iron frame. Photo taken at D on floor plan.

Woodworks of Emeryville, California. The cabinet doors are edgebanded plywood, veneered with vertical-grain Douglas fir—one of our favorite materials for its linear yet subtle grain pattern. Turning the grain direction from one door face to the next can yield beautiful dividends.

Door pulls—I use both positive and negative pulls on cabinet doors. By positive I mean details that project from the surface; a negative pull is an opening in the door. For example, the doors on the coffee-prep cabinet are notched at the corners, creating geometric recesses for the hand and compatible compositions for the eye. Behind the doors, recessed blocks hide the cabinet contents from view. In this case, a block of aniline-dyed bird's-eye maple repeats the color of the bluish concrete (photo bottom left).

On the pantry cabinet, the abstract fish-shaped handle is a Japanese paperweight sliced to form two adjacent handles for the pullout drawers (photo p. 112). On other jobs I have used smooth stones, iron candle holders, fossils, wooden frogs and doll hands for cabinet pulls. I'm careful not to go overboard, though, and usually use only one or two such items in a project.

Steel shelves and a plastered range hood— Thin shelves of cold-rolled ¼-in. steel project from the plastered wall on the stove side of the room (photo p. 112). We gave them a wire-brushed finish and a couple of coats of clear acrylic sealer to fend off rust.

The shelves are affixed to the framing by way of 3-in. wide legs that bend downward at a 90° angle. The legs of each shelf are let into the studs

and bolted. The coral-colored plaster that covers the walls wraps around the hood over the stove (photo above right). Like the shelves, the hood's structure is made of cold-rolled steel. It has an angle-iron frame (inset photo, above right) wrapped on the inside with a stainless-steel plenum assembly that includes a filter and hood lights. Wire lath, spot-welded to the angle-iron frame, serves as the ground for the plaster. We gave it three coats of Structolite (USG; 800-874-4968). We blended the last coat with several iron-oxide based concrete pigments to create the rich, rosy color. □

Fu Tung Cheng is principal in Cheng Design in Berkeley, California. Frank Lee was project architect for the Hertz/Krois kitchen. Photos by Charles Miller.

An Arts and Crafts Kitchen Remodel

A modern kitchen draws inspiration from materials and methods popular at the beginning of the century

by Robert Orr

Older houses have built-in character, but sometimes it takes a tornado to help uncover it. The tornado in this case didn't damage the house, which was built in the 1920s in Hamden, Connecticut, but it did uproot several large trees that had obscured the view of its somewhat plain facade. Dismayed by the loss of the trees, the home's owners asked us to design new porches and a pergola to dress up the newly exposed exterior. This initial encounter, inspired by a natural disaster, eventually led us back into the cramped and dark kitchen.

Our original work on the house had introduced us to its Arts and Crafts elements, including an exquisite copper roof and an interior with handsome wood detailing. But as is often the case, the service section, including the kitchen, was cramped, dark and far less gracious than the rest of the house (photo above). The owners wanted the efficiency and elegance of a contemporary kitchen. But they did not want to have the old kitchen blasted out and a "grand kitchen" inserted in its place, looking as though it had just landed from outer space.

The homeowners wanted the new kitchen to look like it was part of the original house, as if the craftspeople who built the original house somehow could have understood and anticipated in their work exactly how a family would want to live 70 years later. So our design goal was to make something new look as though it had always been there, remaining true to the Arts and Crafts elements that had attracted the clients to the house in the first place.

Same place, before and after. The cramped original kitchen (above) needed a more efficient use of floor space. Reorganizing the original pantry, moving the pantry wall back and recessing the refrigerator into part of the old space eliminates much of the congestion in the new kitchen (facing page). The custom-built, quartersawn oak worktable functions like an island but takes up less room.

Three tricks make a small space seem bigger—Minimal expansion room was available for the kitchen: a tiny breakfast area next to the existing kitchen. Our first priority was to reorient and reconfigure the existing space to make it feel bigger and more elegant.

The first trick was to reorganize some existing features. Straightening out a clumsy pantry/back-hall arrangement and building a recess for the refrigerator created considerable new floor space (photos above, facing page). Without sacrificing any storage area, this new arrangement permits a straight view directly through the house, from front to back, and dramatically eases the tight feeling at this end of the room.

The next trick was to magnify any benefit that could be gained from the breakfast area. By

opening the wall between the kitchen and this area with an arch (photo p. 118), the kitchen feels larger without actually overwhelming the dining space. The arch connects the two spaces while maintaining their individual functions.

The final trick was to capitalize on space elsewhere in the house that might be directed toward the kitchen. Several of the doors and halls on the first floor lined up, although this alignment was not immediately apparent because of a few misplaced walls. Modifying the walls slightly and aligning the new openings in the kitchen and eat-in alcove with existing doorways now visible through the rest of the house make the kitchen feel bigger.

By reorienting existing elements, the room changes from having a claustrophobic inward focus to having an open, expansive outward focus. The new arrangement directs the views past and beyond the kitchen, offering relief from the small size of the space.

Interestingly, the layout of the new kitchen began to resemble the old. The new stove was where the old stove used to be, and the new sink was approximately where the old sink used to be. Apparently, the sink and the stove had worked well in their existing locations for all of those years, but were just cramped by the surrounding space.

Materials are chosen to show the hand of the maker—Characteristic of architects and designers of the English Arts and Crafts movement, such as C. F. A. Voysey and William Morris, is

A simple trick of the eye makes this kitchen appear larger. The aligned entryways tend to draw the eye away from the kitchen and into the rest of the house. This trick makes a narrow kitchen feel larger and less isolated.

what could be described as a celebration of materials, detail and the hand of the artisan.

In this kitchen, the granite countertops are durable and resist stains; their cool mass and dark green/black color balance with the stainless-steel appliances and the oak cabinetry. A double-thick lamination around the nosing edges emphasizes the mass of the stone.

Fulper Glazes (P. O. Box 373, Yardley, Pa. 19067; 215-736-8512) manufactured the ceramic tile used for the kitchen's backsplashes. A prominent 19th-century New Jersey pottery maker, Fulper faded from public view in the 1920s after a major fire. With the discovery in 1984 of six books of glaze recipes in the attic of the family house, three Fulper granddaughters resurrected the business, which now produces tiles based on the original glaze formulas.

All of the cabinets and woodwork are constructed of quartersawn red oak. A popular wood during the heyday of the Arts and Crafts movement, oak was particularly favored for its masculine quality. Rather than presenting the familiar long, bold bands of dark grain typical of flat-sawn oak, quartersawing breaks up the bands of grain into hundreds of tiny flecks of darker color. Glass-front cabinet doors are fitted with locally fabricated leaded glass, and all of the woodwork is protected by a matte finish of catalyzed lacquer.

Utility with design—Another Arts and Crafts detail that inspired the design is high wall paneling, which brings the richness of fine craftsmanship to eye level (bottom photo, facing page). A plate rail 7 ft. 3½ in. above the floor caps the high paneling a small distance below the 8-ft. 8-in. ceiling. Besides crowning the paneling, the plate rail provides ample display space for the homeowners' growing collection of Roseville pottery. An added benefit is that the plate rail resembles a dropped ceiling cornice. The visual effect makes the ceiling appear lifted buoyantly higher, contributing a perception of spaciousness in height similar to the perception created by the three tricks in plan.

At the eat-in alcove the design for the high paneling is interrupted by recessed bookshelves. By heading off a few framing members inside the wall, the bookshelves sit halfway submerged and halfway proud of the wall and provide unobtrusive space for some of the clients' collection of cookbooks.

Furniture also reflects the Arts and Crafts theme—Below the bookshelves, the design for the wall paneling integrates with the design of a wraparound banquette. Built-in seating accommodates more diners in cozier conditions than chairs, and pulling the table away from the center of the room leaves more space for circulation. The covering for the banquette cushions is cut from fabric designed by William Morris, probably the English designer most closely associated with the Arts and Crafts movement. Here, colors and patterns were picked from readily available Morris fabrics to coordinate with the granite counters, the Roseville pottery collection, the paint colors and other materials in the room.

The custom-built dining table was designed to match reproduction Stickley chairs purchased for this kitchen. Constructed from the same quartersawn oak as the rest of the kitchen, the table's top is rounded at the corners to allow for easy slipping in and out of the banquette.

The narrow table in the middle of the kitchen matches the dining table in style and materials. High enough to be a work counter in front of the stove, the kitchen table occupies less area than an island would in this tight space.

Make an asset of a liability—An existing window in the eat-in alcove presented a problem. Probably because the breakfast area commanded the least attention of the house's original designers, its window is positioned well on the exterior of the building but falls in an awkward location inside, a little too high and left of center. The design of the wall paneling imposes a more dominant pattern and distracts attention from the poor location of the window (top photo). As part of the panel design, a new, larger window frame around the existing window centers a new opening on the room. Somewhat proud of the existing wall, the new paneling and frame make the window appear recessed and less important. Within the new window frame, a

Planning and paneling balance an off-center window. This window's asymmetrical placement became an asset in the design of the window seat; the window adds the right amount of interest to the gridwork of the paneling.

A banquette with built-in bookshelves. This nook is pulled back from the flow of traffic, but it's open to the kitchen so that occupants don't feel too isolated from activities there. The dining area unifies many Arts and Crafts themes in the kitchen.

panel grid is set up to balance the window location.

A new window seat and flanking bookshelves and cabinets help to define this space further. The window seat helps make sense of the high sill, and its lift top provides access to practical storage space beneath. By manipulating the panel grid and adding the seat and flanking bookshelves, the window is made to seem desirably offset, adding energy instead of awkwardness to the room design.

Lighting for character and for tasks—It is often better to separate lighting functions so that one kind of fixture is devoted to aesthetics while another handles functional needs. In this kitchen the aesthetics are handled by delicate Arts and Crafts-style pendant lights (Brass Light Gallery, 131 S. First St., Milwaukee, Wis. 53204; 414-271-8300) over the kitchen table and sconces on the wall in the eat-in alcove. With low-wattage bulbs, they give a gentle glow and character to the space, but they don't attempt to meet light-level requirements.

Task lighting is handled by recessed downlight fixtures concealed in the ceiling and by under-cabinet lights above the perimeter work counters. Low-voltage incandescent lamps are inconspicuously placed underneath the base of the upper cabinets, behind the bottom rail. Similar to fluorescent lamps in life span and energy-efficiency, low-voltage lights provide the warm-light quality of standard incandescent lamps and tuck into small spaces.

An artist adds a finishing touch—Central to the Arts and Crafts movement was a collaboration between artisans and artists, a true marriage of every facet of the manmade environment. High on the wall in the band of space between the plate rail and the ceiling, painter Lisa Hess of Stony Creek, Connecticut, was commissioned to design and paint a continuous frieze around the room. In the kitchen she chose a woodland motif appropriate to the natural theme used in all other aspects of the design. In the eat-in alcove she introduced a subtle Garden of Eden theme with the innocent Adam and Eve represented by the clients' two children. □

Architect Robert Orr is the principal in Robert Orr & Associates in New Haven, Connecticut. Photos by Charles Miller.

Center island keeps cabinets off the outside walls. The island contains the sink and lots of cabinet space. Because of its location away from the exterior walls, unobstructed views to the gardens beyond are possible from both the kitchen and the dining room. Photo taken at A on floor plan.

A Kitchen and Dining-Room Combination

An island of floor-to-ceiling cabinets turns one room into two spaces

by Peter Twombly

When I started sketching plans for my parents' retirement house, I laid out the kitchen with the sink on an outside wall and a small counter-height window above. I drew in a peninsular counter toward the dining room and put the stove and the refrigerator on an inside wall. My mother liked this U-shaped kitchen because it provided plenty of counter space and kept traffic circulation out of the work area. As we looked at the sketches, we realized that we probably liked it because it resembled my folks' previous kitchen of 38 years.

Traditional design parameters can be a pitfall to efficient, creative use of space. Regardless of a family's size or lifestyle, many houses still are built with traditional floor plans. And within these floor plans, certain rooms, most notably the kitchens, are laid out the way they always have been. The kitchen sink is on an outside wall and faces a small, above-counter window. And a lot of these floor plans also have redundant spaces, such as both a formal dining room and an eat-in kitchen.

My parents decided against both a formal dining room and an eat-in kitchen, choosing instead to allot part of their construction budget to other amenities, such as a potter's studio for my mother. They needed a room that could serve as both a kitchen and a dining room. It had to be a space large enough to accommodate many guests, but at the same time, my parents wanted the rooms

to be comfortable and intimate when the two of them dined alone.

Rethinking the traditional plan—There were two main problems with the sketch that mimicked the kitchen in which I had grown up. First, because of the peninsular counter, access to the dining room from the kitchen was limited to a single passage, a passage that needed to serve the garage and the potter's studio as well.

Second, the views to the nicest part of the site would be restricted by having the kitchen sink and its row of attendant cabinets run along the outside wall. Granted, there could be a window over the sink, but it would have to be a small window that started above the sink backsplash—around 40 in. off the floor—and this constraint would limit the view. Even if there were to be no upper cabinets over the sink in this plan, I didn't want a short row of stubby windows looking into the gardens. An herb garden, a lily garden, berry bushes and a terrace to the southwest just beyond the kitchen wall are in the landscape plan.

Putting the sink in the island—My solution to both problems mentioned above was to design the counter between the kitchen and the dining area as a freestanding piece of furniture: an island instead of a peninsula. But unlike traditional kitchen islands, this one would have floor-to-ceiling cabinets. I thought of the island as a

Flush drawers and flat-panel doors are understated and elegant. To reduce costs, oak-veneer plywood was used for the door panels and the end of the cabinets. A sliding trash can hides behind the panel to the right of the bank of drawers. Photo taken at B on floor plan.

From the sink there's a view of the dining room and beyond. Although the sink isn't below a window, it is framed by a view into the dining room and the porch. Photo taken at C on floor plan.

Granite counters near the range, plastic laminate elsewhere. Granite makes a great countertop around a stove because of its heat resistance. To the sides of the refrigerator and around the sink, plastic-laminate countertops were used. Photo taken at D on floor plan.

central cabinet, an oversize breakfront that would allow the kitchen and dining room to occupy one room while allowing each space its own identity.

This central cabinet would solve the aforementioned traffic problem; people could circulate around the cabinet from either side. Thus, someone working in the kitchen could get to the dining area without blocking the passageway to the garage and the potter's studio.

By putting the sink and dishwasher in the central cabinet, we freed the exterior wall along the southwest side. And the problem of the restricted views outside was solved: From anywhere in the kitchen or dining room, my parents could look outside to the beautiful gardens though the series of tall casement windows. Another advan-

tage to clearing the exterior wall of all of the kitchen cabinets was that conventional baseboard heating could be used rather than noisy kick-space heaters.

What results is a dining room-kitchen combination, separated by only the island cabinet, that functions well for everyday use with easy access for food serving and dish clearing. The floor-to-ceiling cabinet also provides enough screening between the two areas to minimize views of dirty dishes and food preparation from the dining room during more formal meals.

A recessed refrigerator makes space in the kitchen—For the most part the kitchen and dining room is enclosed by four perimeter walls, forming a large 26-ft. 3-in. by 15-ft. rectangle. The

range cabinets and the telephone desk are built on the inside of a perimeter wall. But the cabinets and counters that housed the refrigerator posed a problem.

I didn't want these cabinets to extend inside the perimeter of the room because it would have meant losing 2 ft. of the width of the kitchen space. Losing that 2 ft. would have required moving the door to the garage and to the potter's studio as well as losing 2 ft. from the length of both the island and range cabinet.

The solution was to borrow 2 ft. of space from the front-hall stairwell on the other side of the kitchen. Recessing the refrigerator and its flanking cabinets into the wall gave me the needed space for the rest of the kitchen. The front edge of the refrigerator and cabinets is in a straight line

Small photos above: Jefferson Kolle

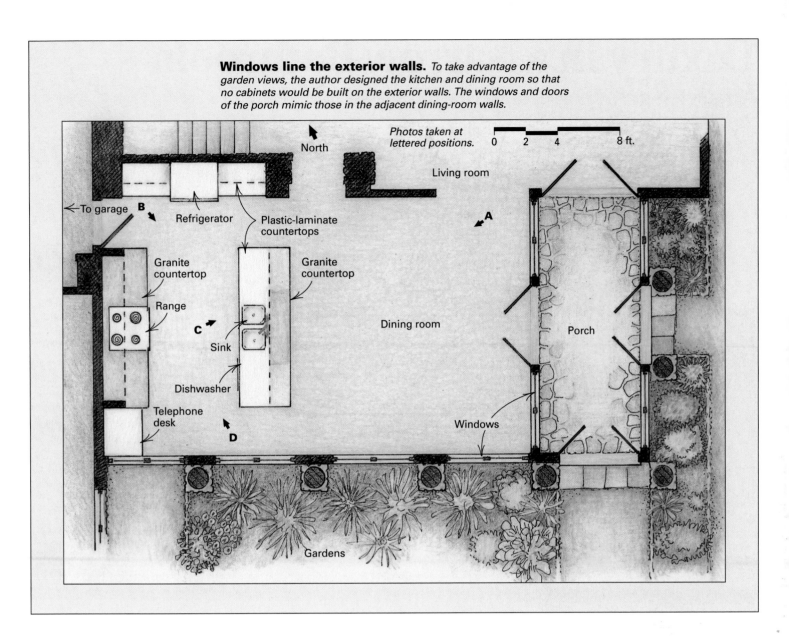

Windows line the exterior walls. *To take advantage of the garden views, the author designed the kitchen and dining room so that no cabinets would be built on the exterior walls. The windows and doors of the porch mimic those in the adjacent dining-room walls.*

North

Photos taken at lettered positions.

0   2   4   8 ft.

Living room

To garage   **B**

Refrigerator

Plastic-laminate countertops

A

Granite countertop

Granite countertop

Range

Dining room

C

Sink

Porch

Dishwasher

Telephone desk

D

Windows

Gardens

---

with the perimeter wall of the dining room. Another advantage of the recess is that there is a straight-line passage from the dining room into the studio and the garage.

Pass-through cabinets with glass doors let in light—Along with the sink and dishwasher, the kitchen side of the island contains storage drawers and cabinets for all the dishes and utensils. Serving dishes and table linens are kept in the cabinets and drawers on the dining-room side of the island.

Although there is not a glazed window above the sink as is the convention in most kitchens, the space above the sink is framed by the opening in the island between the kitchen and dining room (top right photo, facing page). One can stand at the sink and talk with guests at the dining-room table and look beyond the table, through the porch, to the outside.

To increase light, visibility and access, the upper cabinets have glass doors on both sides. The dishes can be taken from the dishwasher on the sink side, put into the cabinets, and then for setting the dining table, the dishes can be removed from the dining-room side.

Different countertops for different uses—From the island, the kitchen evolved into a simple three-part design. As mentioned, the sink and the dish storage are in the island. The second part is the food-preparation area. It's on the wall opposite the island, and it includes the range, microwave and storage for pots and pans. The third station, also on an inner wall, houses the built-in refrigerator and food-storage cabinets (drawing above).

A granite countertop surrounds the range, providing a place for rolling out dough and for setting down hot pans with impunity (bottom right photo, facing page). On the kitchen side of the island, I used plastic-laminate counters. They're considerably less expensive than the stone, and my mother wanted the lighter appearance of the laminate around the sink.

There is another small section of granite counter on the island's pass-through between the dining room and the kitchen. The idea is that a hot vessel can be taken from the oven or stove and placed on the pass-through countertop for serving in the dining room without burning the counter. On the small counters flanking the refrigerator, we used plastic laminate.

Custom tiles and handy dish towels—All cabinets, trim and flooring in the kitchen and dining room are red oak. The ceiling is native red oak 8x8 beams and tongue-and-groove cedar decking. To achieve a simple, informal look, the cabinets have flat-panel doors with butt hinges and tapered 1-in. wood-block pulls (left photo, facing page). To dress up the cabinet doors on the dining-room side of the island, the cabinetmaker, Kevin McCullough, applied a cross-shaped batten to the wide panels (photo p. 120).

All backsplashes are custom tiles stenciled in an abstract pine-needle pattern to match painted frieze panels in the adjacent living room. Custom light fixtures are a combination of antique and reproduction shades and standard brass components found in the Bowery of New York City.

On both sides of the sink, towel bars are recessed into the cabinets. Drying dish towels are hidden from both the dining room and the sides of the cabinets, yet they are within easy reach of the sink.   □

Peter Twombly is an architect with Estes & Company Architects in Newport, R. I. Photos by Boyd Hagen except where noted.

Luxury in a Narrow Bathroom

A frameless glass door separates the tub and shower from the rest of the room

by Peter Feinmann

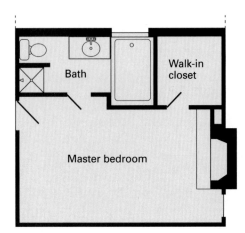

Before

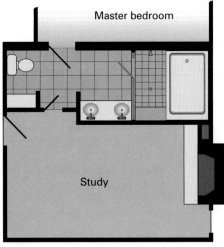

After

Lose a closet, gain a spa. *Space for the shower/tub combination was gained by annexing a former closet. Although the resulting space is long and narrow, the tempered-glass enclosure and frameless shower door avoid claustrophobia by fostering a sense of spaciousness.*

Life sometimes demands a slow lane. Commuting and managing family life made my clients desperate for a retreat in their 80-year-old country home near Boston. Originally a one-room hunting shack, the house had undergone a series of major renovations over the years, but one problem remained: the dark and cramped master bath. It was utilitarian, but it offered little in the way of luxury.

Extra room comes from the closet—During the home's most recent renovation, a new master bedroom and master bath, designed by a local architect and the owners, were added to the house. The old master bath was barely large enough to accommodate two adults, much less do it comfortably, especially during the morning rush. But because the new master bedroom had room for a new walk-in closet, we were able to steal space from the former closet and incorporate it into the new bath (drawings left). This made the bathroom considerably bigger, but in the form of a narrow room a little over 5½ ft. wide and almost 22 ft. long.

Moving the existing whirlpool tub and reinstalling it at the far end of the bathroom created an additional 3½-ft. by 5-ft. shower area with room for a built-in seat and simple and safe access to the tub (photo facing page).

The high sloped ceiling helps to prevent the long, relatively narrow room from feeling like a shoe box, and leaving the existing wood beams and rafters exposed also suggests the feeling of spaciousness. An electrically operated 2½-ft. by 4-ft. skylight (Andersen Rv2944V, Andersen Windows; 800-426-4261) directly over the vanity lets in fresh air (when wanted) and natural light. A quiet bathroom fan (Nutone QT, Nutone; 513-527-5100) helps to minimize mildew and moisture problems and ensures good ventilation during long New England winters.

A frameless shower door opens up the bath—It is difficult to include both a bath and shower in a long, narrow space without creating a claustrophobic corridor. The solution turned out to be creating a spacious wet area at one end that would combine both bath and shower functions, yet still leave plenty of room for a double-sink vanity, toilet and linen closet in the other end. A frameless ⅜-in. tempered-glass door let us do this work without turning the bathroom into a cave.

These types of doors are expensive, typically costing between $2,000 and $3,000 for this type of installation, but in this bathroom the added sense of spaciousness was well worth the added cost. These enclosures look simple—that's part of their appeal—but tempered glass is unforgiving. After it's made, you can't trim it, drill it or notch it, so everything has to be just right the first time. The door installation is one responsibility that I was quite happy to delegate to a specialized glass fabricator.

The shower area has an integral seat topped with Corian to match the vanity countertop. The seat provides a safe spot to sit down and relax while taking a shower. The shower floor has an off-center drain that keeps it from being underfoot and is covered with glazed terra-cotta 6-in. by 6-in. floor tiles that contrast with the larger wall tiles.

The shower head by Hans Grohe (Grohe America; 770-844-7414) is mounted on a track and has a removable spray handle. Tall and short people can find a comfortable showerhead height, and the removable handle makes it a lot easier to clean the shower and the adjoining whirlpool tub. □

Peter Feinmann is a designer/builder and the owner of Feinmann Remodeling in Arlington, Massachusetts. Photo by Steve Vierra.

Step on in. A tempered-glass enclosure and frameless shower door separate the tiled tub and shower area from the rest of the bathroom but don't stand in the way of the view. A built-in shower seat, rustic beams and a view into the trees contribute to the bath's sense of serenity.

A Bigger, Better Bathroom

Tile, glass block and solid-surface material make a dramatic, light-filled bath

by Lee Moller

One night during the construction of Mark Levine and Arlene Kaufman's master bathroom, Arlene called and complained about hot water coming from cold-water taps throughout the house. The toilets were a little warm as well. It turned out that earlier that day, the plumber had installed the shower valves. One of the valves was left open, but with the shower outlet capped off, no water was running. The open valve allowed the house's hot water and cold water to mix slowly.

In spite of this little plumbing snafu, we eventually were able to give Mark and Arlene what they were after: a master-bedroom suite that would be a private place to spend time together. Their wish list for the master bathroom included a large shower, a large spa tub and lots of storage space. The master bedroom before the renovation was of adequate size, but closet space was minimal. And the adjoining bathroom was small, dark and dated.

Fewer, more spacious rooms—We began the design process with the intention of keeping all four upstairs bedrooms in the suburban Denver trilevel home. But after we looked at several layouts, it seemed clear that in order to include a big tub, a big shower, a big vanity and more closet space in the new suite, one small bedroom would have to go. Because their children are grown, Mark and Arlene decided they could sacrifice one small bedroom.

We moved the new master bathroom into an existing small bedroom and closet area that measured 10 ft. by 13 ft. We also took a few sq. ft. of space from the hall and eliminated a hall closet, giving us another 139 sq. ft. to work with. Under the new floor plan, the master bathroom would occupy 188 sq. ft., the bedroom 179 sq. ft., and closets 87 sq. ft. The main bedroom closet would be double its original size. In all, the new suite would occupy 454 sq. ft. (floor plan right).

Window defines the bathroom layout—Everything in the bathroom was laid out along an 8-in. by 8-in. grid that was aligned with an existing window (photo right, facing page). The depth of the vanity, the elevation of the tub

A private, spacious master bathroom. *In a suburban Denver home, a bedroom was eliminated to create the space for a new master bathroom. The pocket door separates the bathing and dressing areas from the master bedroom.*

Storage cabinet

Glass-block wall

Vanity

Medicine cabinet

Pocket door

Bedroom

Spa tub

Shower

Walk-in closet

deck, the location of the shower wall, the location of the shower valves and heads, and the location of the glass-block walls all were based on the grid. The 8-in. dimension started with the glass block and allowed us to make fewer tile cuts. The actual dimension of the glass block is 7½ in. by 7½ in., with a ½-in. mortar joint.

We replaced an aluminum sliding-glass window with an awning window. We put two courses of glass block under the replacement unit. This configuration allowed for privacy, fresh air

and ample natural light. We installed a Hurd awning window that fit the opening and worked with our grid (Hurd Millwork Co. Inc., 575 S. Whelen Ave., Medford, Wis. 54451; 800-433-4873). For strength and for rigidity, we added a 4-in. header to go between the glass block and the window.

To help give the new bathroom a spacious feeling, we decided on an open shower that requires no door or curtain and has two shower heads (photo right, p. 129). The tub deck and shower seat were built on site and covered with ½-in. Corian (E. I. DuPont, Chestnut Run Plaza, P. O. Box 80702, Wilmington, Del. 19880; 800-426-7426), finished with a routed ¼-in. bullnose edge. The Corian deck worked nicely with the curved bathtub deck design.

Corian caps the glass-block walls—We chose Italian glass block in a wavy pattern (Fidenza Vetroarredo, Glass Block Unlimited, 126 E. 16th St., Costa Mesa, Calif. 92627; 800-992-9938) (photo left, p. 129) for the glass walls because of its clear color and distorting characteristic. The Italian material is free of the green tint common in other brands of glass block.

To make the 90° outside corner where the back and side shower walls meet, we used glass corner blocks from the same manufacturer. The corner blocks, unlike the square blocks of the main wall, were available only in a smooth, non-wavy finish. We decided to use them anyway and were pleased with the result.

The stepped, glass-block shower wall was capped with ½-in. Corian, the same thickness as the mortar joints (photo left, p. 129). Corian proved to be an ideal material to finish the stepped glass block. To make the caps, we cut the Corian to the same width as the blocks and then glued it to the glass with clear silicone. Inside and outside corners of the ½-in. stock were fit tightly and then fused with a Corian seam kit. The entire cap received a slight roundover, using a ¼-in. radius router bit. Final grouting was done after completion of the Corian work.

Corian also was used for the spa-tub deck and the shower-area curb cap. The material can be cut easily into curved shapes and provides an

Drawing: Dan Thornton

"The tilesetter thought I was nuts." The author cut each tile by hand with nippers in order to achieve a smooth, natural fracture line. The rough tile edge was finished in place with two coats of appliance touch-up paint.

Yes, that wall is finished. Some tile clearly was needed at the master bathroom's east wall, but the homeowners wanted space to display a work of art. The author suggested the fractured-tile idea as an alternative to a standard geometric pattern.

easy-to-maintain horizontal surface. The shower shelves were laminated from three pieces of Corian, one ½ in. and two ¾ in. thick. The shelves were anchored with ½-in. by ½-in. Corian splines, attached to the framing with 2½-in. screws. The Corian shelves, sloped down slightly for drainage, then were fused to the splines.

Three different tiles work in concert—We used three types of tile for the bathroom, all with matte finishes: a 7¾-in. by 7¾-in. white finish Portobello for the walls (Portobello America, 470 West Ave., Stamford, Conn. 06902; 203-961-8070); Graniti Fiandre gray-brown 8-in. by 8-in. tile for the floor (TransCeramica LTD, 1159 Bryn Mawr, Itasca, Ill. 60143; 800-828-9074); and an American Olean 1-in. by 1-in. unglazed porcelain mosaic tile (in the color the company refers to as "stone") for the shower floor and the bathtub's curved deck face (American Olean Tile Co., 1000 Canon Ave., Lansdale, Pa. 19446; 215-855-1111). The Portobello wall tile works with the dimensions of the grid. The Fiandre floor tile was chosen for its fine granular quality and matte finish. We set it at a 45° angle to relate to the entrance and to contrast with the orthogonal grid. The 1-in. unglazed mosaic provides a welcome change of scale, and it also worked well for the curves.

Unglazed porcelain tiles are most often seen in commercial bathroom installations and around swimming pools, but they work well for residential applications. The 1-in. unglazed mosa-

one was plenty. By using only one sink, we were able to add another bank of drawers in the cabinet space below, an option that Arlene preferred. We managed to fit 18 drawers in the 14-ft., 10-in. vanity. The vanity top is Corian with a 1½-in. bullnose edge and a Corian integral bowl.

A cabinet made to fit the space—The medicine cabinet is located in a small triangular space that was part of the original hall. We made the medicine-cabinet door by gluing a ¼-in. mirror to ¾-in. birch-veneer plywood. Heavy-duty European 40mm, 160° hinges help keep the heavy door from sagging.

This medicine-cabinet door happened to swing under a recessed-can light fixture. If the cabinet door were left open under the light, heat from the light could be sufficient to ignite the door and cause a fire. Heavy-duty nylon shock cord (available from a mountain-climbing or marine supplier) and eye hooks were installed for a simple but effective way to keep the door from remaining open under the light.

Fractured-tile wall—One evening late in the project, I faxed over several elevation sketches of possible east-wall tile layouts. The original idea was to step down the tile on the east wall, repeating the pattern of the glass-block shower and toilet-partition walls. But Arlene didn't like this or any of the other geometric possibilities for ending the tile on the east wall. The couple didn't want to tile the entire wall because they wanted a place where they could hang art in their new bathroom. Also, an all-tile wall would have been boring.

The last drawing I faxed that evening contained the fractured-tile idea (photo left, p. 127), inspired by my love of the Colorado mountains. After some debate, we decided to do it. The fractured-tile design was transferred from an elevation drawing to the wall with a grease pencil. The tiles were rough-cut first with a tile cutter, and then they were nibbled away to their final form with tile nippers.

The cutting process was slow and painstaking. My fingers were sore and blistered after eight hours of slowly nibbling away at tiles. When I did a similar fractured-edge finish in granite at my own home, I used a 7¼-in. dry-diamond masonry blade mounted to a circular saw for the first cuts. A 4-in. diamond blade mounted to a small grinder or a wet saw does well for the final work. Nippers don't work well with hard materials such as black granite.

Hand tool produces the right look—For tile, nippers give a nice, smooth, natural fracture line, a finish difficult to achieve with the abrasive action of speeding diamonds. If I were to do this type of project again, I would use dia-

More storage space was part of the program. By eliminating one of two sinks originally considered for the long vanity, the homeowners got an extra bank of drawers below.

ic tile comes in 1-ft. by 2-ft. sheets that bend easily. They're ideal for shower floors because they conform well to drainage slopes and because of their slip-resistance.

To carry the increased floor loads from the new spa tub and the glass-block walls, we doubled the floor joists under the bathroom.

A long mirror above a big vanity—The most important requirements for this project were spaciousness and lots of storage space. Running the bathroom mirror from the backsplash to the ceiling for the length of the vanity creates a spacious appearance and interesting reflections of the space (photo above). Moisture wicking up behind a mirror can damage the silver reflective material and create ugly black lines in the mirror. To prevent damage, we applied a generous layer of silicone between the bottom of the mirror and the backsplash.

Because the longest mirror available to us was 12 ft. and because our wall was nearly 17 ft., we decided to create a corner medicine cabinet at one end and a 3-ft. wide floor-to-ceiling cabinet at the other. Although there was plenty of room for two sinks we had envisioned, we decided

A seamless approach to capping a glass-block wall. The strips of Corian that make up the wall cap were carefully fitted and then chemically welded at the joints. The ½-in. Corian was chosen to match the thickness of the grout lines between glass blocks.

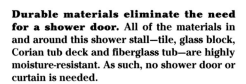

Durable materials eliminate the need for a shower door. All of the materials in and around this shower stall—tile, glass block, Corian tub deck and fiberglass tub—are highly moisture-resistant. As such, no shower door or curtain is needed.

mond grinders for defining rough-edge shapes in the tile, then finish the cuts with the nippers. Tile nippers, while they create a clean fracture line, have a tendency to cut more than intended. If you try this look, be prepared to waste a few tiles.

The fractured edge was finished with a couple of coats of glossy, durable touch-up paint made for appliances. We tried glazing the jagged edges of test pieces by applying a ceramic glaze and firing the pieces, but we were unhappy with the results that we got. The sharp edges of the tile did not retain the glaze well, and the color of

the bisque tile showed through. By using appliance paint after the jagged tiles were set, we eliminated the long process of glazing, firing—and waiting.

A projector aimed at the wall with a slide of a favorite horizon is a good way to create a fractured-wall pattern. Rugged mountain ranges make some of the best subjects.

Folks viewing Mark and Arlene's new bathroom for the first time have commented on the openness, the inviting bathtub, the huge shower and all of the cabinet drawers. But after seeing the fractured-tile wall, some have asked, "What

happened?" or "Is it done yet?" The tilesetter thought I was nuts when I informed him of the plan. Mark wasn't sure about it when he first saw it, but Arlene liked it from the get go. The jagged wall provides a pleasing reprieve from the grid and a playfully fractured finish to an otherwise ordered design. The original notion was to provide a space on this wall for a piece of art. What better solution than to make the wall a work of art itself? ☐

Lee Moller is a designer and general contractor in Denver, Colorado. Photos by Jefferson Kolle.

A Comfortable Cottage Bathroom

Painted wainscoting and a shower window transform a simple bathroom into a cozy, elegant space

by Kathie Wheaton

It's not uncommon that a folder full of pictures torn from magazines puts the architect in the role of pasteup artist rather than designer. So I was pleasantly surprised when my clients presented a six-page written program for their new home, which included specific ideas for their master bathroom. They liked the cottage feel of vertical, beaded wainscoting, but they wanted to maintain some of the formality of their urban lifestyle. An easy-entry shower with a seat and a view was at the top of their wish list.

A small bump-out creates a larger space—The main body of the master bath measures only 8 ft. by 14 ft., so we bumped the window wall out 2 ft., making the bathroom feel much larger by adding only 14 sq. ft. of extra floor space (floor plan right).

Ordinarily, windows in a shower area are a recipe for disaster, but we made the frames and sills for these awning windows out of Corian (inset photo, facing page). The solid-surface trim piece between the windows continues to the floor. The rest of the shower is tiled except for a Corian bench angled into the outside wall. The pan for the shower was recessed into the floor to minimize the threshold for easy access.

Beaded paneling unifies cottage theme—Starting at the shower enclosure, white-lacquered wainscoting (made of tongue-and-groove material called beadboard) wraps around the room and across the face of the tub enclosure (photo facing page). White tiles continue the wainscot's line around the tub to form the splash. Towel bars in the tub and shower are actually ADA-approved grab bars with a white finish by Pressalit (American Standard, P. O. Box 90318, Richmond, Va. 23230-9031; 800-223-0068).

On both sides of the vanity, the beadboard extends to the ceiling and forms columns that frame the vanity mirror. A cabinet is built into each column with doors held closed by touch latches. Drawers below the vanity top continue the line of the columns to the floor. The vanity-top surface is laminate, but we used solid surface for the edge to withstand hair-dryer and curling-iron abuse and to eliminate the black line at laminate edges.

We also used soffits over the perimeter areas of the bath. The lowered ceiling defines specific areas of the bathroom such as the tub and the shower and makes these spaces more intimate. The soffits also house recessed lighting fixtures and give the room a better sense of proportion.

The clients capped off the cottage feel with wallpaper in an ivy pattern. The soft greens and the white background of the paper complement the crisp white of the beadboard and cabinetry, and the ivy plant on the window ledge of the shower provides a visual link to the trees outside. □

Kathie Wheaton is an interior architect working with James Barnes Architects in Providence, Rhode Island. Photos by Roe A. Osborn.

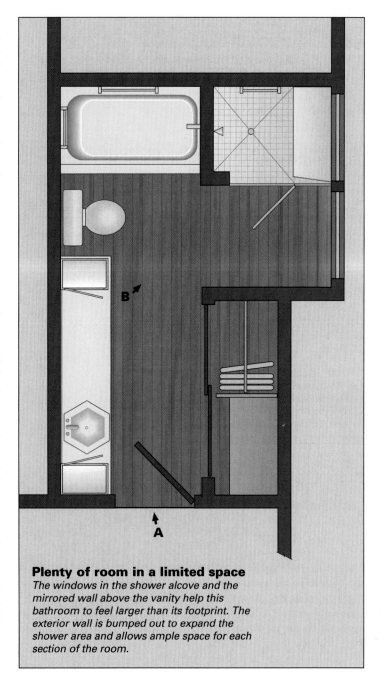

Plenty of room in a limited space
The windows in the shower alcove and the mirrored wall above the vanity help this bathroom to feel larger than its footprint. The exterior wall is bumped out to expand the shower area and allows ample space for each section of the room.

Drawing: Dan Thornton

Personal privy with a private view. Arranged in a tight L-shape, the areas of this compact but intimate bathroom are tied together with beaded pine wainscoting. Corian-trimmed windows that are in the shower area (inset photo) overlook a secluded backyard. Photo left taken at A on floor plan; inset photo taken at B on floor plan.

A Craftsman-Style Writing Alcove

This home office has traditional detailing and thoughtful spaces for modern tools

by Alan Jencks

I was finishing up a window-seat project when she came over from next door. Her name was Judy, my clients' neighbor. Judy asked if I would be willing to do a little job, fixing a door hinge. I said I'd see what I could do.

The following day I went to have a look and found the door barely hanging on. I fixed the door, and now, five years later, Judy and I are married. So in part this is a story about how a bad hinge led to a wonderful relationship. But mostly this article is about building a place where Judy can write and grade papers. In addition to writing poetry, Judy also teaches English and creative writing to inner-city high-school kids.

During our first meeting to discuss the writing alcove, Judy introduced me to the house—a 1½-story, 1,800-sq. ft. 1908 vintage Craftsman bungalow with a shingled exterior. The entry, the living room and the dining room are paneled two-thirds height in rich, dark Douglas fir. The public rooms are topped with massive crown moldings, and the bedrooms and the baths are finished in plain plaster and drywall (a 1960s remodel) with some simple moldings and trim.

Judy wanted to locate the alcove in the rear of the house, where it could overlook the garden (photo right). The logical place to put the alcove was in the bedroom closest to the backyard. This space originally was a long, narrow screened porch. But even though it was on the southwest corner of the house, its small, aluminum windows kept the room dark. A multilite door joined this room with another tiny bedroom. Despite the windows, the overall feel of both rooms was cramped and gloomy. Adding to the claustrophobic feeling, there was no access to the backyard from these rooms and no view of the rose garden outside.

Getting the most out of a small space—Judy and I first spoke generally about the kind of space she wanted. It had to be light, open, simple, elegant and functional. Because the space

The bay bumps into the garden. The writing alcove extends beyond the line of the original house, supported by wooden brackets that were bandsawn to resemble the flowers of the nearby trumpet vine. Redwood V-rustic siding wraps the bay. The Port Orford cedar post next to the door doubles as the door's jamb.

had to serve as study and bedroom and because the individual rooms were small, we decided to combine them. At first we thought it best to separate the writing alcove and the bedroom with a couple of French doors. But that plan changed in a dramatic way. When I learned that Judy spends a good deal of time at the ocean, an arched opening, shaped like a wave or a seashell, seemed a perfect way to link the rooms (top photo, p. 134). Her love of the sea and things nautical also influenced the use of natural finished wood, capturing the warmth and intimacy of a wooden ship's cabin.

Judy wanted a doorway to the garden, so

placement of the desk (photo facing page) was pretty much dictated by the L-shaped space available. The corresponding L-shaped bay window for the desk seemed an obvious solution, saving floor space, providing a view of the rose garden, good natural lighting and plenty of desktop space for poring over her students' homework.

The L-shaped window projects 15 in. beyond the south and east walls. By popping out the bay, we gained 70 cu. ft. of building space: enough for windows and storage space at the back of the desk. If furniture were set up to approximate the desk area and functions, it would have required more space.

The height of the window ledge above the desk was based primarily on the largest item going in the desk, a Mac LC computer. The depth of the window ledge is equal to the distance Judy can reach comfortably while standing at the desk. If the ledge were deeper, it would be difficult to keep it clean and to water the plants on it. Other dimensions, such as the desk height off the finished floor (28 in.) and the height of the pull-out keyboard tray (25 in.) are standard.

To emphasize the outline of the window bay, I dropped the ceiling over it 5 in. For the same reason, I lowered the ceiling over the desk 2 in. In addition to accentuating the lines of the bay and the desk, I think the stepped ceiling gives the space a more intimate feel.

Judy and I laid out the desk details together. She sat at her old desk, and we arranged things within reach and tried to keep the most frequently needed items close to the seating position. The computer is centered, with the phone and the answering machine on the left to keep her right hand free to write. The tape player and the CD player are left of the phone, with pigeonholes for tapes and CDs above. On the short leg of the desk, we located pigeonholes for stationery, paper, stamps and envelopes. To the right of the computer, we placed a letter-size file drawer, which was a compromise location—it

A place for everything. The computer monitor tucks into the space under the window ledge, centered between a file drawer and a stack of pigeonholes for electronic components, tape storage, envelopes and miscellaneous office supplies.

opens over the desk surface. It would have been handy to have it below desk height on the right, but I thought it would appear bulky hanging down, breaking the clean, horizontal line of the desk. A hanging-file drawer also would restrict legroom. Two under-desk drawers were planned, but eventually Judy and I omitted them for the same reason. The two ends of the desk back are angled toward the seating position so that reference books are easy to see and select.

Judy also needed more closet space, so I added one diagonally opposite the desk, a few feet away. The closet's proximity to the desk gave me an idea. Why not tuck the laser printer in there? I'd thought about locating the printer somewhere on the desk, but that strategy presented a lot of problems. The printer switch is inconveniently located on the back of the machine, and loading paper and changing the toner cartridge require considerable space and frequent access. Putting the printer in the closet solved those problems.

I put the printer on a ¾-in. plywood shelf that is supported by a four-drawer file cabinet. I found a 25-ft. eight-pin printer cable that I ran under the floor from the computer to the printer. The cable made it with barely 2 ft. to spare. If you're contemplating a similar printer setup, be aware that some printers can be hooked up to the computer with four-conductor phone wire.

Detailing the bay—To accentuate the open feeling around the desk, I angled the sides of the bay 45°. The angled sides face the neighbors, so to preserve some privacy, I glazed these side windows with tulip-pattern glass, which is frosted glass with some wiggly, clear veins in it.

The two large windows over the desk hang on horizontal pivots. The windows open outward at the bottom, providing plenty of ventilation while open only an inch or so. There are no curtains or shades over the windows. Occasionally, when the sun is too strong, Judy shades the seating area in front of the computer with a cedar screen placed on the window ledge. On the exterior, the new windows are protected at the top by a copper shroud that is mounted just below the rain gutters (top drawing, facing page).

I used several species of softwoods to achieve a warm, complex straw color. The ceiling is paneled with 1x4 V-groove T&G hemlock. The windows, the desktop, the pigeonholes and the baseboard are clear Port Orford cedar. The door casings and window casings are sugar pine and Alaskan cedar, and the door-head casings are Douglas fir. The doors are Douglas fir and sugar pine. The floors have been left as they were, white oak strip, resanded and finished with polyurethane.

Linked by an arch. A wall with a sweeping curve defines the line between the bedroom and the adjacent writing alcove. The angled sides of the bay window and the multileveled ceiling frame the alcove, imparting a sense of intimacy.

Wall brackets hold up the desktop. Tapered 4x6s affixed to the wall framing eliminate the need for legs under the desk. The keyboard rests in the retractable tray, fed by the coiled wire that disappears into the wall.

Opening up the bay—As a remodeler, I often have misgivings when I have to dismantle a finely crafted old detail to make way for new construction. But no pangs of guilt tugged at me when I tore out the aluminum windows at the back of Judy's house. You could almost hear the house breathe a sigh of relief when the windows hit the Dumpster.

Along with the windows, I took out the headers and trimmers that supported the second-floor framing. The loads are now carried by a 5-in.

steel I-beam in the wall over the computer (top drawing, facing page). To maximize the window height and preserve the roofline, I had to use the shallowest header possible. Steel was the answer. I affixed the beam to its posts by way of bolts run through mounting flanges that are welded to the beam. On the backyard side, the I-beam cantilevers beyond the corner post to pick up a short section of header that carries the roofing over the bay bumpout. I framed the bay with kiln-dried hem fir to minimize shrinkage problems, and just to be on the safe side, I glued the studs, the blocking and the brackets together with construction adhesive.

The bay assembly sits on top of a sheet of ¾-in. fir plywood. The plywood is screwed to the top plate of the stud wall and it is supported beyond the line of the foundation by seven brackets. Craftsman houses throughout Berkeley are distinguished by their hand-wrought wooden details, and the brackets that hold up roofs and bay windows frequently get some special attention. I tried to stay within that tradition by cutting a sweeping curve into the bottoms of the brackets, which are made of 3x12s. Then, I cut V-shaped grooves into the tops of the 3x12s to receive the 4x4s that carry the bay. I used a bandsaw to cut the flower shapes into the ends of the 4x4s.

Making the desk—A substrate of 1-in. birch plywood spreads loads on the desktop. The finished top is ½-in. by 7-in. Port Orford cedar, edge jointed, then glued and screwed to the plywood substrate. I finished the cedar top (and all the adjacent woodwork) with ProFin, a hard-drying oil finish (Daly's Inc., 3525 Stone Way N., Seattle, Wash. 98103; 206-633-4200).

The desktop is supported by five tapered 4x6 cedar brackets (bottom photo, left). Each bracket is screwed and glued to the framing and blocked along its sides and bottom.

Pigeonholes fit between the window ledge and the desktop. When laying out pigeonholes, it is essential to have all of the various components on hand. For items of a consistent size, such as tape cassettes, you can make the storage slot pretty tight. Just leave enough room to get a finger in to pry one out.

If electronic components are to fit into the pigeonholes, make sure you've got the devices on hand, including instructions and service manuals. A simple cable connection can cause problems if you don't know where it has to occur.

It's also important to know how much room is required to operate a component. For example, an answering machine may be only 6 in. wide and 3 in. high, but you may need a 10-in. high opening with a light so that you can see what you're doing and have room to push the buttons.

For power I ran a plug strip behind the pigeonholes. Made by Wiremold (Wiremold, P.O. Box 10639, West Hartford, Conn. 06110-0639; 800-621-0049), the plug strip has outlets every 6 in. The strip is on its own circuit, as is the computer. Because Mac computers are switched on and off from the rear, I plugged the computer into a switched outlet. The switch is under the window ledge above the screen so that one can reach above the computer to turn it on and off.

Ambient lighting is provided by a series of recessed tube-light strips tucked under the window-ledge molding. Task lighting is from above, where three low-voltage recessed fixtures are mounted. I chose the low-volt lights because they take up little room and because their inconspicuous trims don't detract from the ceiling. The MR 16 50-watt lamps I chose put out plenty of candlepower. Near the arched partition, a pendant fixture is mounted over the reading chair.

Building the arch—The most enjoyable aspect of the project was building the wave-shaped archway—not only because it was a welcome departure from straight lines but also because the curve imparts a wonderful rhythm and movement to the space. I started the curved opening by installing a 7-ft. 4x10 header to carry the floor load above. Then I tacked a two-piece ¼-in. plywood template over one side of the opening. On this template I drew the arch free-hand because it seemed a better way to generate a curve that had a natural arc to it, instead of the formulaic, trammel-controlled curves that, to my eye, have a man-conquers-nature feel.

I laid the template onto a couple of sheets of ¾-in. furniture-grade maple plywood, traced the profile and cut it out with a sabersaw. Then I sanded the edges smooth. To improve the plywood's dimensional stability, I sealed its sides and edges with an oil-based sealer.

I started building the wall by tacking the plywood for one side in place. Then I built a stud wall that follows the contour of the arch. The 4x4 post next to the passageway through the arch extends into the floor framing, stiffening the wall. I glued and screwed the plywood to the studs, which turned the whole assembly into a box beam with an arc cut out of its middle.

I used a rabbeting bit in my router to mill the plywood's edges. The rabbeted edges allowed me to recess expanded metal lath between the plywood skins (bottom drawing, right). I covered the lath with a coat of 40-minute joint compound. Then, I applied a second coat of standard joint compound. I tooled this layer with a sheet-metal template I cut to register against the plywood. This left a uniform, curved profile.

I taped the seams in the plywood with paper drywall tape. Then I skim-coated the entire wall with all-purpose joint compound. Finally, I finished the wall by lightly sanding it, priming it once again with an oil-based sealer and then rolling it with flat latex paint. □

Alan Jencks is a designer and general contractor in Berkeley, Calif. Photos by Charles Miller.

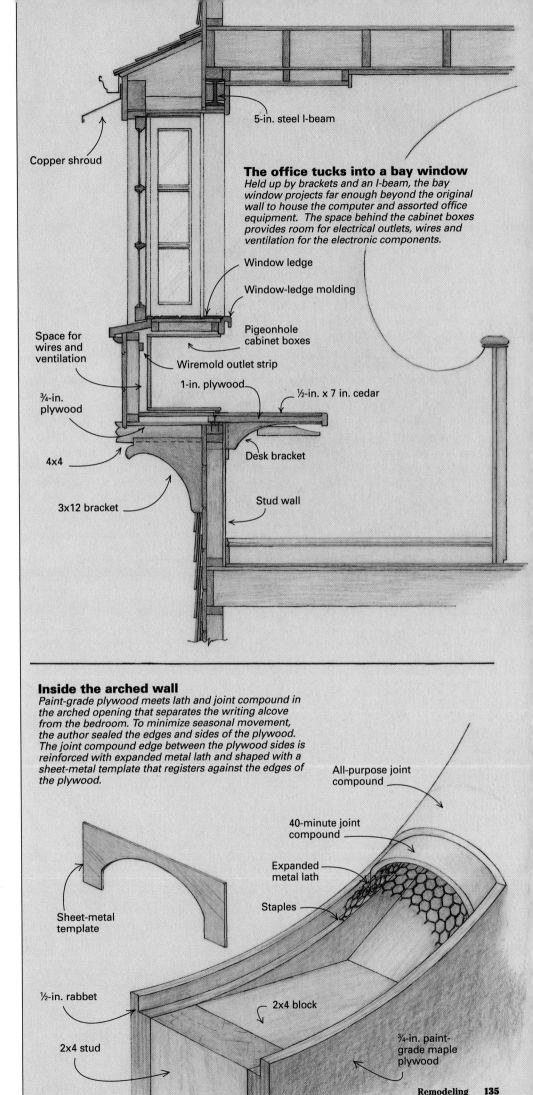

The office tucks into a bay window
Held up by brackets and an I-beam, the bay window projects far enough beyond the original wall to house the computer and assorted office equipment. The space behind the cabinet boxes provides room for electrical outlets, wires and ventilation for the electronic components.

Copper shroud

5-in. steel I-beam

Window ledge

Window-ledge molding

Space for wires and ventilation

Pigeonhole cabinet boxes

Wiremold outlet strip

¾-in. plywood

1-in. plywood

½-in. x 7 in. cedar

4x4

Desk bracket

3x12 bracket

Stud wall

Inside the arched wall
Paint-grade plywood meets lath and joint compound in the arched opening that separates the writing alcove from the bedroom. To minimize seasonal movement, the author sealed the edges and sides of the plywood. The joint compound edge between the plywood sides is reinforced with expanded metal lath and shaped with a sheet-metal template that registers against the edges of the plywood.

All-purpose joint compound

40-minute joint compound

Expanded metal lath

Staples

Sheet-metal template

½-in. rabbet

2x4 stud

2x4 block

¾-in. paint-grade maple plywood

Facelift for a Loft

A curved wall, choice materials and a light-conscious design bring two rooms to life

by Richard Ayotte

It's not uncommon in New York City to find oddly shaped living spaces. They're usually the products of half-successful attempts at converting old industrial buildings and warehouses into living spaces. A recent project of mine involved such a space: a cramped, awkwardly arranged bathroom in a duplex loft apartment. The adjacent room—a dark, inhospitable space—didn't improve the livability of the apartment. My firm's task was to provide a more open space, rework the bathroom and create a casual sitting area that could double as a study. Making rooms feel bright was a key element of the program. Also, budget constraints dictated that the sauna and the apartment's

electrical panel remain in place. Though we were free to relocate the existing whirlpool, we had to reuse it as well as isolate its motor acoustically in order to address complaints from the downstairs neighbors.

Design solutions—The apartment's owners wanted to minimize any awkwardness in having the main bathroom next to what is a public, social area. They also wanted to move the entrance to make it less conspicuous from the sitting space. We studied several possibilities, with an eye toward disguising the room's function when viewed from without. The solution was a curved wall between the two

rooms, flaring open to an enlarged entry area (drawing facing page). The wall's sensuous shape helps to soften the otherwise small, rectilinear spaces, and the glass block in the wall allows some passage of light between the rooms without compromising privacy (photo facing page).

We hoped to create a sense of expansiveness by creating an ordered, visually uncluttered space, so it was important to integrate all the disparate elements in the bathroom and to open up the floor space as much as possible. For example, the whirlpool bath was moved to the far corner of the room and set between existing walls to minimize its impact.

A habitable space. White walls, glass block and track lighting above the bookshelves serve to lighten the sitting area and create a feeling of relative spaciousness in a small room. *Photo by Charles Wardell.*

Traditionally free-standing elements, such as the vanity, were built in for the same reason. Mirrors were added to cover the walls over both the whirlpool and the vanity to expand the space visually. A custom towel rail hugs the wall, emphasizing its curve. Tile and accent colors are carried throughout the room (photo right).

Building in apartment buildings—As is typical with projects in apartment buildings, work was restricted to the apartment's interior, without recourse to access from adjoining apartments. Also, major plumbing lines had to remain in their existing locations, and work hours were kept from 9:30 to 4:30, weekdays.

The building has only one small elevator, which meant that many of the materials had to be walked up—six floors. The large bathroom mirrors proved especially difficult; we broke more than one en route up the fire stairs.

Inherited headaches—Construction problems, particularly in buildings originally designed for nonresidential use, can be complex. While the original structure may be sound, and accurate plans may exist for it, subsequent owners do not always document changes. To compound the problem, workmanship on these changes is often shoddy. Most of our difficulties were caused by such renovations.

Shortly after our contractors, Supply Side, Inc., began demolition, we discovered that the original bathroom ceiling, which we had wanted to keep, was supported on a metal stud partition we wanted to remove. It should have been suspended from the building structure, as the New York City Building Code requires. This necessitated additional demolition and new construction, not to mention the largest change order for the project.

Installing the new plumbing lines proved problematic as well. Although we didn't know the exact locations of joists, we thought we could assume (based on the orientation of the finish wood flooring) that they'd be perpendicular to the flooring. As it turned out, we discovered during demolition that the wood strip flooring had been installed over an earlier finish floor, and perpendicular to it. Resulting design changes were insignificant, but additional time was required to complete the more circuitous plumbing runs.

A custom shower base—The existing shower, which we were replacing, had a ceramic tile floor

Bright and open. To open up the bathroom visually, the contractors relocated the whirlpool and replaced the wall between the sitting area and the bathroom with a curved wall. *Photo by Vincent Laurence.*

set on a raised plywood base. Movement in the base, due either to inadequate structural support (causing excessive deflection) or to delamination of the plywood from repeated wettings, had resulted in frequent cracking of the grout. This had required nearly constant maintenance to prevent water leakage to the apartment below.

To avoid a recurrence of this problem in the new shower, we had planned to install a prefabricated cast-stone base. Unfortunately, we couldn't find a stock base to fit the odd-size space in which we had to work. Rather than alter the shower layout at this stage, we built a new plywood base and reduced the joist spacing beneath it to 12 in. o. c., thereby virtually eliminating deflection. Over the plywood, we placed a continuous layer of Bituthene (W. R. Grace Company, 62 Whittemore Ave., Cambridge, Mass. 02140; 800-242-4476), a rubberized membrane material used to waterproof roofs, walls and foundations. We ran the membrane up the walls approximately 12 inches to act as a "flashing," and down into the central drain to prevent any chance of leakage at the point of exit. Ceramic tile was installed over the Bituthene, using a mud base and thinset adhesive.

A close call—The most significant work delay we experienced involved one of our basic materials—the ceramic tile. The speckled, tan-colored porcelain tile intended for the flooring and some walls was impervious to water penetration, had excellent slip-resistance, and made a good color match with the existing whirlpool bath. The sole New York distributor assured us that the German manufacturer could deliver the quantities needed in plenty of time to meet our schedule. The contractor placed his order and put down a 50% deposit. Well into construction, the tile distributor vanished in apparent bankruptcy. All of the rough construction and fixture placement had been completed to accommodate the metric-sized tile. Consequently, switching to a readily available American tile would have incurred considerable additional work and compromised the quality of the project.

Fortunately, one of the apartment's owners, Richard Winger, was fluent in German and was able to speak directly to the manufacturer, who provided the tile for the balance that was owed on the order. □

Richard Ayotte is a principal in the firm Richard Ayotte Architecture in New York City.

Floor plan: after (detail)

Whirlpool — Shower

Vanity

Up

Bedroom

Electrical panel

Sauna

Floor plan: before

Shower — Vanity

Up

Whirlpool

Bedroom

Electrical panel

Bedroom

Sauna

A garage becomes a library. A coffered ceiling constructed of kiln-dried spruce wrapped in oak is an elegant finishing touch for a library that had been a two-car garage. Ceiling panels of MDO plywood are painted before they are installed in the grid of beams and purlins.

A Simple Coffered Ceiling

Common materials turn a garage into an elegant library

by Fred Unger

Dana Carter can thank his wife's love of plants for the comfortable library where he now indulges a passion of his own—books (photo above). The library might have remained one of those idle daydreams if Sonja had not become the president of her garden club after she retired. Soon afterward, Sonja's plants were competing for room with Dana's ever-expanding collection of books. It wasn't long before Sonja suggested they build a greenhouse.

The Carters brought me in to help plan this addition to their Rhode Island home. As we talked, the project expanded. After looking at several possible sites around the house for the greenhouse, we decided it would be built on the east

Beam meets purlin. The purlins are made by wrapping 2x6 spruce in ¾-in. thick oak. They are then cut to length and installed between the main beams.

side of their existing two-car garage. The garage would be turned into a potting room and library, and then a new garage would be built next to it. Sonja's simple greenhouse project was quickly turning into the largest remodeling project my company had ever undertaken.

The 14-ft. by 24-ft. library took shape after my crew repaired the concrete slab, framed the new wooden floor and built interior walls that would separate the library from Sonja's work area. Oak bookshelves and cabinets were designed to give Dana plenty of book storage, and this new room was crowned with a coffered ceiling constructed with common materials: 3/4-in. red oak, 1/2-in. medium-density overlay (MDO) plywood and kiln-dried framing lumber. A simple building technique and a mitering jig made from plywood helped us complete the ceiling on site.

The ceiling takes shape—The coffered ceiling is similar to one that my crew and I had built in part of our showroom. The ceiling consists of a grid of main beams and purlins (smaller, intersecting beams) capped on the bottom with 3/4-in. thick oak strips whose edges have a beaded profile (bottom photo, p. 138). Once the beams are made, the MDO plywood is cut to fit openings in the grid, painted white and dropped in.

When the Carter's garage had been built, collar ties were run across the room about 2 ft. above the level of the top plates. That's where we installed fiberglass insulation. We extended the insulation and vapor barrier between the roof rafters down to the walls at the perimeter. This left a warm space and a little working room above the level of the new library ceiling. Should people need to work overhead later (to run wire or ductwork, for instance), they won't have to wrestle with fiberglass batts to get there.

Before the interior walls were closed up and plastered, we installed 2x8 kiln-dried spruce joists across the 14-ft. width of the library. These 2x8 joists were installed a few inches below the top plates of the walls and spaced about 4 ft. apart. The joists—which would become the main ceiling beams when we were finished—were screwed to the sides of studs and are supported from below with jack studs (top drawing, left). We face nailed 2x8 spruce ledgers to the wall studs between these joists, then nailed 2x8 ledgers across the end walls as well. The result was a grid of spruce 2x8s whose bottom edges had been leveled.

Once the basic framing was in place, we finished the rough ins and insulation and then plastered the walls so that we wouldn't have to clean up the oak face pieces and trim later. Once the plastering was out of the way, the next step was to glue 3/4-in. thick by 5-1/2-in. wide oak to the sides of all the joists and to the faces of the ledger boards all the way around the room. We used mostly glue to avoid a lot of unnecessary nail holes in the stock and to provide a rigid finished beam. The bottom edges of the oak pieces were brought slightly below the bottom of the spruce framing so that when the cap pieces were added later, the bottom edges of the 2xs wouldn't prevent a tight fit.

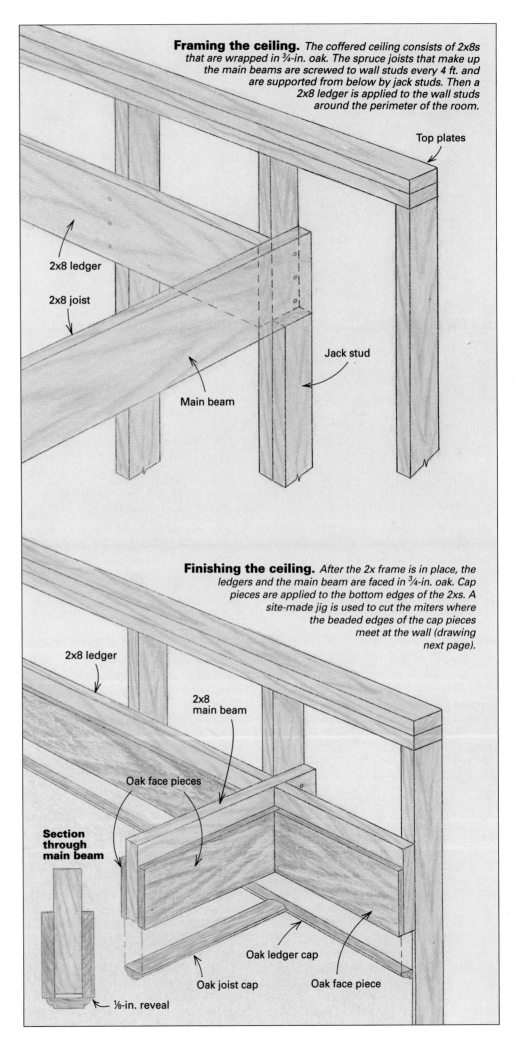

Framing the ceiling. *The coffered ceiling consists of 2x8s that are wrapped in 3/4-in. oak. The spruce joists that make up the main beams are screwed to wall studs every 4 ft. and are supported from below by jack studs. Then a 2x8 ledger is applied to the wall studs around the perimeter of the room.*

Top plates

2x8 ledger

2x8 joist

Main beam

Jack stud

Finishing the ceiling. *After the 2x frame is in place, the ledgers and the main beam are faced in 3/4-in. oak. Cap pieces are applied to the bottom edges of the 2xs. A site-made jig is used to cut the miters where the beaded edges of the cap pieces meet at the wall (drawing next page).*

2x8 ledger

2x8 main beam

Oak face pieces

Section through main beam

Oak ledger cap

Oak joist cap

Oak face piece

1/8-in. reveal

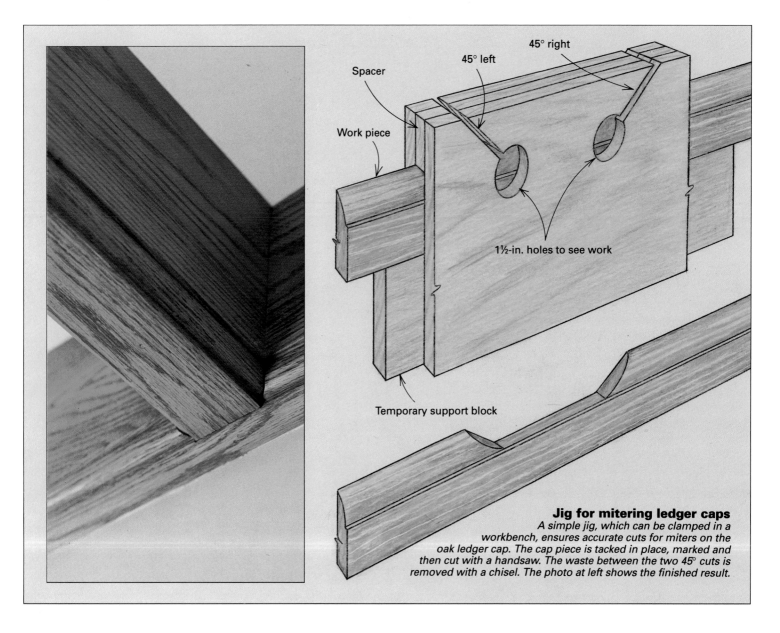

45° left

45° right

Spacer

Work piece

1½-in. holes to see work

Temporary support block

Jig for mitering ledger caps
A simple jig, which can be clamped in a workbench, ensures accurate cuts for miters on the oak ledger cap. The cap piece is tacked in place, marked and then cut with a handsaw. The waste between the two 45° cuts is removed with a chisel. The photo at left shows the finished result.

The sides of the joists above the oak face became stops for the MDO plywood that would be dropped in later.

Capping the bottom of the beams—With the joists and the ledgers faced in oak, we installed the ledger cap pieces, then the joist cap pieces spanning the room.

We began by milling the ¾-in. thick cap pieces, 1¾ in. wide for the ledgers and 2¾ in. wide for the bottom of the joists. The cap pieces are slightly narrower than the oak-faced joists and ledgers, allowing a ⅛-in. reveal on each edge. We used a ⅜-in. ball-bearing beading bit in a router to dress one edge of the ledger cap and both edges of the beam cap pieces.

Where the joists and the ledgers intersect at the wall, the edges of the cap pieces had to be mitered (bottom drawing, previous page) while the bodies of these pieces were butted. It wasn't as hard as it looked. First, we tacked up the oak cap pieces on the two walls perpendicular to the joists. With those cap pieces temporarily in place, we used a scrap of the joist cap to mark the ledger cap piece where it had to be mitered. After each joint had been marked, we took the ledger cap pieces down and used a simple miter

jig (drawing above) to make the two 45° cuts with a handsaw. We chiseled out the waste between the two cuts and back beveled the cuts to ensure a tight fit. Then we installed the ledger cap piece with glue and nails. The mitering jig, which is about 3 ft. long, didn't take long to make and was designed to be clamped to a workbench when we needed it.

With the ledger cap pieces installed, all that remained were the joist cap pieces. The corresponding miters at the wall intersections for those pieces could be cut on a chopsaw. We left these pieces a hair long to ensure a tight joint. Then the joist cap pieces were glued and nailed in place (photo above), which completed the basic structure of the ceiling.

Purlins and panels—While installing cap pieces, we also were gluing up the purlins—2x6 kiln-dried spruce wrapped in ¾-in. by 3½-in. oak. These had oak cap pieces nailed and glued on their bottom edges, and the assemblies were left long. When the glue was dry, the purlins were cut in a 15-in. miter saw so that they fit snugly between the sides of the main beams. While held snugly in place with bar clamps, the purlins were toenailed with a pneumatic finish nailer through

the oak, then screwed through the spruce from above with long wood screws.

The installation of the purlins created rectangular holes that we filled with the ½-in. MDO plywood. MDO plywood has a resin-treated paper surface, making the face smooth and giving it excellent painting characteristics. After the plywood panels had been cut to size, we glued a 1x4 strip of pine on edge to the back of each panel so that it wouldn't sag over time.

After we finished building the ceiling, interior doors and trim were installed, and the painters took over. The ceiling panels were painted white while the oak ceiling trim and all the oak doors and casings were stained and urethaned. When everything was dry, the panels were simply dropped in to rest on the top edges of the oak face pieces like commercial drop-ceiling panels. The spruce center of each framing member stuck up high enough to keep the panels from sliding around. And because the panels were painted before they were installed, we didn't have to ask painters to cut all those edges later. □

Fred Unger runs Heartwood Building Specialties, a design and building company, in Berkley, Mass. Photos by Scott Gibson.

Index

The articles in this book originally appeared in *Fine Homebuilding* magazine. The date of first publication, issue number, and page numbers for each article are given at right.